FAITH AND BEAUT

'Aesthetics' and 'theological aesthetics' usually imply a focus on questions about the arts and how faith or religion relates to the arts; only the final pages of this work take up that problem. The central theme of this book is that of beauty. Farley employs a new typology of Western texts on beauty and a theological analysis of the image of God and redemption to counter the centuries-long tendency to ignore or marginalize beauty and the aesthetic as part of the life of faith.

Studying the interpretation of beauty in ancient Greece, eighteenth-century England, Jonathan Edwards, and nineteenth- and twentieth-century philosophies of human self-transcendence, the author explores whether Christian existence, the life of faith, and the ethical exclude or require an aesthetic dimension in the sense of beauty. The work will be of particular interest to those interested in Christian theology, ethics, and religion and the arts.

Faith and Beauty

A Theological Aesthetic

EDWARD FARLEY
Vanderbilt University, USA

Ashgate

Aldershot • Burlington USA • Singapore • Sydney

Published by
Ashgate Publishing Limited
Gower House
Croft Road
Aldershot
Hants GU11 3HR
England

Ashgate Publishing Company
131 Main Street
Burlington VT 05401-5600 USA

The author has asserted his moral right under the Copyright, Designs and Patents Act, 1988, to be identified as the author of this work.

British Library Cataloguing in Publication Data
Farley, Edward
    Faith and beauty : a theological aesthetic
    1. Aesthetics – Religious aspects – Christianity
    I. Title
    230

Library of Congress Cataloging-in-Publication Data
Farley, Edward, 1929-
    Faith and beauty : a theological aesthetic / Edward Farley.
        p. cm.
    Includes bibliographical references.
    ISBN 0-7546-0453-5 -- ISBN 0-7546-0454-3 (pbk.)
    1. Aesthetics--Religious aspects--Christianity. 2. Aesthetics. I. Title.

BR 115.A8 F37 2001
230--dc21   00-054278

ISBN 0 7546 0453 5 (HB)
ISBN 0 7546 0454 3 (PB)

Printed and bound in Great Britain by MPG Books Ltd, Bodmin, Cornwall

Contents

Preface

An autobiographical note may help explain how this work on theological aesthetics had its origin. I had almost completed a rather comprehensive interpretation of the Christian faith when I realized there was something odd about that project. The oddity was the tension – one could say, lack of relation – between the way in which I had interpreted the Christian faith and one of my own strongest orientations. From as early as I can remember, I have been fascinated by the sights, colours, occurrences and sounds of everyday life. Childhood memories of the smell of the Kentucky river at dawn and the sweet sadness evoked by certain strains of music are still with me. To say this is to claim nothing distinctive for myself. I would guess that most children are moved by the mysterious attractions of what seems to them to be an enchanted world. This lifelong, intense, precognitive relation to things was never a mere processing of information. Rather than being value-neutral, indifferent or dull, its tone was one of fascinated interest – a positive participation in a primordial attractiveness that was not derived from other sorts of values. In other words, it was aesthetic.

The oddity of my theological project was that it almost entirely ignored this powerful aesthetic dimension of my actual life.[1] It was as if the most concrete way in which human beings experience their world – namely, their emotional participation in surprising, interesting and attractive events – had no place in the world of faith. Faith, it would seem, is simply about 'something else': church doctrines, the after-life, Jesus, the Bible, liberation. This odd lack of relation between faith and the aesthetic dimension of human life is not, I realize, peculiar to my project, a rare autobiographical idiosyncrasy. It haunts the work of most theologians I know. It was only after finishing a four-volume work on Christian theology that I was prompted to inquire into theology's typical exclusion of the aesthetic from faith and, beyond that, the place of the aesthetic in the life of faith.

Three terms in the book's title help express what this project is and is not about: aesthetics, beauty and faith. The term, aesthetics, has come to mean a philosophical account of the arts that exposes and clarifies the canons of art criticism.[2] Accordingly, the term 'theological aesthetics' suggests a theology of the arts – an account of the place of the arts in the worship and life of the community of faith. I am not inclined to repudiate the importance of such an inquiry. In this work, however, 'aesthetics' refers to a dimension of human experience, an engagement with and participation in what is intrinsically attractive – in other words, with what is beautiful. Some readers may baulk at the word 'beauty'. Certainly, it is an unfashionable concept in aesthetics, art criticism and the arts themselves. But from Plato through Kant to Whitehead, beauty has been the term used to describe something about the world (harmony, differentiation, novelty) which if experienced at all gives some sort of satisfaction. In this meaning of the aesthetic, a theological aesthetics uncovers the relation between what is intrinsically attractive and the life of faith.

The word 'faith' does not lend itself to precise definition. It can mean belief in, trust, the doctrinal content of Christianity, a contrasting word to 'works', and many other things. In this book it is the inclusive term for the mode of existence that comes with redemption. The life of faith has communal and individual aspects, both of which ensue from redemption or, one could say, grace. The question that launches this inquiry, then, is whether and how such a mode of existence is in any sense beautiful and whether and how it gives rise to sensibilities to beauty. The thesis of the book can be simply stated. Beauty is intrinsic to the life of faith because it is a feature of the divine image which is distorted by sin and restored by redemption. Unfortunately, the route to this simple thesis is historically and philosophically circuitous, which is why I have appended a synopsis of argument.

Despite recent complaints about an excessive preoccupation with method in at least some forms of theology, it is best always to give at least a minimum account of how one approaches theological inquiry. The reader will not find in this work the more rationalistic kind of cognitive style which posits some privileged premise – a doctrine, for instance, and deduces its way to a conclusion. Such a procedure is not without its advantages and contributions – for instance, the disclosure of a doctrine's implications. The reason why I do not work that way is that I am persuaded that theology's first moment is not a specific doctrinal theme but a very compact and multisided state of affairs, the actuality of redemption. Gathered into the fact of redemption – always already there so to speak – are all of faith's specific motifs: human evil, Spirit, creation, divine image, grace, God, Christology, ecclesia. Furthermore, if redemption is historically and personally actual, the world (nature, society, persons and so on) is never simply external to it. Redemption is something that takes place in the world and that means the world is ever a part of it. Comprising and shaping what redemption transforms are the workings of nature, human biological life, cosmic structures and the dynamics of economic and political institutions. Theology must unpack this compact, historical density whenever it tries to display the concrete actuality and the transforming content of redemption. Accordingly, the method of this inquiry is partly historical – that is, it attempts to identify several principal ways in which Western texts have understood beauty – and partly constructive – that is, it tries to discover how faith or redemptive existence is open to, and even embodies, these various senses of beauty. The method is more ecological (it would uncover interdependent systems at work in a complex phenomenon) than linearly deductive.

It is impossible to complete a work of this sort and not fail to recognize its limitations. Clearly, the historical studies are more suggestive than definitive. What concerns me more is the impoverishment that inevitably attends any work that restricts itself to Western or at least post-Hellenic philosophical, religious and aesthetic traditions. There is a rather obvious rationale for limiting a theological inquiry to the intellectual heritage of Europe. Christianity originated as a Hebraic faith taken up into, and thus co-opting, the cultural worlds of Mediterranean peoples. Hellenic, Hellenistic and Roman thought and culture shaped Christianity's self-interpretations almost from the outset. Hence, the story of beauty in the Christian movement is largely a Western story. On the other hand, beauty occupies a central place in many of the world's faiths, such as Hindu, Buddhist and Native American. The Christian movement does have some presence in the East and thus has found interpreters who approach it more from Eastern than Western angles. Eastern and Native American peoples do have very distinctive ways of understanding the relation between beauty and the sacred. Surely, a Christian theological aesthetic would profit from dialogue with these traditions? The absence of that dialogue is a serious limitation of this inquiry.

Even within its framework of the Western story of beauty, another set of limitations calls for qualification and supplementation. My treatment of the texts of beauty slights a tradition I do not know very well and for which beauty is very important – the textual and liturgical tradition of Greek and Russian Orthodoxy. Furthermore, within the Western story of beauty, there are suppressed and marginalized religious and ethnic traditions of beauty that have little or no public textual expression. Is there, for instance, an African-American tale of beauty that contains a distinctive notion of beauty's pathos and a distinctive history that does not coincide with the principal Western paradigms of beauty? Is beauty in any way affected by gender experience? Do women experience beauty (as some say they experience knowledge) in a different way from men? These are only a few of the many differentiations of beauty and its interpretation that are part of the Western tale of beauty. Many of these specific traditions and lines of cultural experience are stories yet to be told, paradigms still to be uncovered. Without doubt, this treatise would be far more adequate if its theological appropriations could have engaged both the broader scene of religious faiths and the more differentiated traditions of the West.

Some readers will discern another limitation. The most widespread and influential type of Christian theology on the planet may well be some form of praxis or political theology. These theologies continuously remind us that human suffering born from social oppression is so massive, so intense, so poignant that it must take precedent over all other claims upon us. In the face of the ethical and political need to address the conditions of suffering, all other matters seem trivial, superficial and self-serving. How dare starvation and homelessness still plague our planet? Edna St Vincent Millay says about love what we could also say about beauty.

> Love is not all: it is not meat nor drink
> Nor slumber nor a roof against rain . . .
> Love cannot fill the thickened lung with breath,
> Nor clean the blood, nor set the fractured bone.[3]

I can only grant the point. The ethical has a certain primacy. The question I raise in this inquiry is whether the ethical excludes beauty, whether the withholding of beauty itself fosters certain dehumanizations and oppressions.

This project originated in two invitations to give public lectures. One came from by my own school, the Divinity School of Vanderbilt University, to give one of the Cole lectures. The other was the invitation to give the Ferguson lectures at the University of Manchester in England. I fear that this work retains very little of the actual text of these lectures, but these invitations did provide the occasion for me to explore what had been a lacuna in my own past writings. I am grateful to the faculty and to Dean Joe Hough for the Vanderbilt invitation and to Professor David Pailin, my host at the University of Manchester.

Notes

1   The omission is not total. Beauty and wonder hover on the edges of my study of evil and redemption. See *Good and Evil: Interpreting a Human Condition* (Minneapolis: Augsburg Fortress, 1990), pp. 164, 205–8.

2   'Aesthetics' was originally coined by the German philosopher, Alexander Gottlieb Baumgarten in *Reflections on Poetry* (1735) and *Aesthetica* (1750). By way of the term, Baumgarten called for a new science distinct from both logic (formal rules of thinking) and natural sciences, that would inquire in a disciplined way into sensory experience. But almost immediately after Baumgarten, the term was broadened (hence G.F. Meier, 1748), for it is just at the point of pre-logical experience, of nature for instance, that human beings experience their world not just as a set of quantities but as pleasing, beautiful. And this sort of experience is, at the same time, at the root of the experience of music, art and poetry. Thus, aesthetics was quickly linked with beauty and also with the arts. The eventual result of this turn, manifest in textbooks and reference works on aesthetics, was that the arts (or theory of the arts) came to define aesthetics. Typical interpretations in these works do leave some place for beauty in the definition of aesthetics. Nevertheless, the primary definition of aesthetics in the textbooks is a philosophy or theory of the arts. Beauty is part of the definition insofar as the authors see the arts themselves as containing an element of beauty. For instance, see 'Aesthetics' in *Encyclopedia Britannica* of 1929. As the twentieth century proceeded, beauty became more and more marginal to aesthetics, primarily because it is being expunged from the arts themselves. Thus, the *Encyclopedia Britannica* (Chicago: University of Chicago, 1992) can say that aesthetics is 'the theoretical study of the arts and related types of behavior and experience', observing that beauty is only one of many motifs gathered up into artistic experience. Almost all contemporary textbooks on aesthetics define the term as philosophy or theory of the arts. For a history of the term, see 'Aesthetik', in Joachim Ritter and K. Grunder (eds), *Historische Wörterbuch der Philosophie*, Vol. I (Basel/ Stuttgart: Schwabe and Co., 1971). Eberhard Jüngel is one of the few late twentieth-century writers to retain Baumgarten's definition, thus defining aesthetics as 'the theory which treats of that which is perceived (as true) and more precisely that which is *perceived as beautiful*': 'Even the Beautiful Must Die', in *Theological Essays II*, trans. A. Neufeldt-Fast and J.B. Webster (Edinburgh: T. and T. Clark, 1995), p. 62.

3   Edna Saint Vincent Millay, *Collected Poems* (New York: Harper and Row, 1956), p. 659.

Chapter 1

Beauty as the Beast: Traditional and Postmodern Expressions

...no longer loved or fostered by religion, beauty is lifted from it face like a mask. (Hans Urs von Balthasar)[1]

Protestantism – the adroit castrator
Of art; the bitter negation
Of song and dance and the heart's innocent joy –
You have botched our flesh and left us only the soul's
Terrible impotence in a warm world. (R.S. Thomas)[2]

This book is about beauty, a topic no longer central in the 'high' arts, philosophy (including aesthetics), *belles lettres*, culture studies or (Western) religion.[3] This does not mean that beauty has been successfully expelled from the world, culture or human experience, which is very difficult to do, as the next chapter will argue. Rather, beauty is only rarely part of the postmodern *episteme* – that is, the taken-for-granted societal consensus about what is important and what is real.[4] Beauty has ceased to be an important notion both in discourses that interpret 'the way the world is' and in discourses that express primary human values – those of human experience, the arts, ethics and religion. Western postmodern societies more or less understand themselves, what they are about and the world at large without it. Indeed, they are able to conduct their politics, worship, education and even arts without that notion. This chapter has a modest aim – namely, a brief account with only a minimal explanation, of this discursive absence, this cultural and religious disinterest in beauty. Further, I offer this account without attempting a precise definition of beauty, a task I put off to a later chapter.

In the old French tale, Beauty is initially repulsed by the Beast. By eliminating it from the discourses of interpretation, postmoderns turn Beauty into the Beast. As the Beast, beauty is idolatrous, seductive, effete, amoral, elitist, essentialist and quaint – 'an ornament on the bourgeois past', as Hans Urs Von Balthasar says.[5] A variety of discursive devices can bestow a beastly status on a selected cultural symbol or value, thus rendering it irrelevant, discredited or linguistically invisible. One way in which a term can undergo conceptual and cultural discreditation is by opposition to another term that has self-evident importance or validity. By way of the rhetorical device of dichotomy, a term is located on the 'bad' side of a column and thus in polar opposition to the 'good' term. Thus arise discursive dualisms that place beauty (and sometimes even aesthetics) on one side, moral good (and religion) on the other. In opposition are beauty versus faith, beauty as hedonism and aestheticism versus the real world of suffering, oppression, and politics or, in more deconstructive mode, beauty as reference, meaning and sobriety opposed to difference, novelty and play.

Because the roots of beauty's beastly status are multiple, and in some cases very old, a serious account (a Nietzschean genealogy?) of these roots calls for extensive inquiry into the texts and institutions of Western history. I shall take up this task only in the most minimal way, assembling some selected evidences for beauty's discursive suppression. I do this in the three areas of present-day postmodern culture, Christian religious piety and Western Christian theologies.

Beauty and the Postmodern

Over 50 years ago, Simone Weil left us with a devastating picture of modern beautyless societies:

> Today one might think that the white races had almost lost all feeling for the beauty of the world, and that they had taken upon themselves the task of making it disappear from all the continents where they have penetrated with their armies, their trade, and their religion.[6]

Her complaint was both a lament at the end of an era and a glimpse of what was to come – a summation of a 150 years' long movement that we now call the 'modern' and sometimes 'romanticism'.

These cautionary movements were protests and holding patterns against the powerful economic and cultural shifts that finally produced the postmodern. The theme of beauty is prevalent in nineteenth-century European literature, poetry, painting and the arts. Aesthetic theory incorporated beauty into its very definition and self-understanding.[7] But throughout the period of the modern, beauty rapidly disappeared as an important motif in itself and as a way in which Western peoples experience and interpret the world. And this is why both 'romanticism' and 'modernism' have elements of cultural nostalgia.[8] Nostalgic are the lines from one of the late Romantic poets:

> No soft Ionian laughter moves the air,
> The Thames creeps on in sluggish leadenness,
> And from the copse left desolate and bare
> Fled is young Bacchus with his revelry.[9]

Protested here is the kind of society and even the kind of human being that walked onto the stage of human history with the Industrial Revolution. The nostalgia is for a pre-industrial, pre-urban, immediate relation to nature. The 'modern' then paradoxically included both the new industrialized societies with their new economics, politics, modes of warfare, population growth, and urban culture, and the nostalgic *ressentiment* against these things.[10]

In using the term 'postmodern', one faces not only the many meanings that have now gathered around the term, but a primary ambiguity.[11] According to Jacques Derrida, Jean-François Lyotard, Charles Jencks and others, the postmodern refers to a certain *orientation* at work in a variety of late twentieth-century undertakings (physics, architecture, art, literature, philosophy), an orientation that understands itself to be a departure from the *modern*. On this side of the ambiguity, we find a second division of meanings. A postmodern orientation can be primarily idealizing and utopian – that is, a departure from the modern that understands itself to be redemptively iconoclastic and liberative. Here, the postmodern means a societal resistance to, a 'detoxification' of, modes of thinking (foundationalism, reality reification, essentialism) that serve as instruments of past and present oppressive regimes and *epistemes*.[12] On this idealizing side, detoxifying postmodernism retains important continuities with the protests – romantic and otherwise – that arose with the modern. On the 'realistic' and less idealizing side of the postmodern is an orientation that is more or less indifferent to societal transformation. Here, the postmodern understands itself as radical criticism and departure (again, in philosophy, literary criticism, the arts) which in extreme form would eschew discourses of reference, value, reality, depth, presence and meaning. At work in various cognitive and cultural locations, this postmodernism is anti-structure, anti-subject, differentiating and playful.[13] In the sense of an orientation, the postmodern is an identifiable movement *in* culture, something going on in universities, academic fields, various arts and other cultural practices such as law. It resides in the studio, the concert hall, the classroom and, possibly, the laboratory.

On the other side of the ambiguity, the postmodern refers not to something *in* culture (an interpretive elite, for instance) but a culture-wide shift. The 'postmodern' describes what happened, historically and culturally, to the 'modern'.[14] Historians, social scientists and philosophers such as Frederic Jameson, Christopher Lasch and Jean-François Lyotard track the way in which contemporary industrial (or post-industrial) societies of the West have departed from the modern. For the most part, this is not a utopian literature. The 'postmodern turn' may have destabilized the conventions and institutions of both the premodern and the modern that created gender and other hegemonies, but what came with these destabilizations had little or no liberative or redemptive interest. Postmodern *culture* names what happens to art, religion, morals, education, governments, leisure and entertainment and everyday life when commodification, consumerism and the secondary mediations of 'spin' communication replace all the 'deep symbols' – that is, prevailing cultural values and all gender, ethnic, regional and religious identities which in the past were the bearers of moral consciousness. In this sense, the postmodern is both a development and epoch of recent history and also a human type beset by multiple identities, bombarded constantly by an all-pervading marketing machine, and alienated from the immediacies of nature, the deposits of wisdom in human traditions and the interdicts that arise with communities of personal relations.[15] The postmodern tends to displace conventional loyalties, appeals to value, and strong convictions with multiple interpretive schemes.[16] Because this multiplicity destroys the whole order of representation and the real, thus the conditions for self-transcending criticism, the postmodern is an anti-aesthetic 'culture of narcissism'.[17]

Despite the power and popularity of these accounts, we need not conclude that the 'postmodern turn' (cultural narcissism, plurality of psychological identity, and radical relativism) utterly dominates all the human beings and institutions of late twentieth-century societies. Much still goes on in these societies that looks and feels very un-postmodern: popular religion, little changed from the nineteenth century, remnants of older aesthetics, antiquated cultural undertakings, various fundamentalisms, ethnic stabilities and even cultural isolations. Huxley's 'brave new world' (the postmodern) may have arrived but the traditional 'natives' still live and work in its cities. Thus, a truly comprehensive account of turn-of-the-millennium Western societies needs to explore how and why premodern and modern strands persist in the postmodern turn. The two senses of the postmodern – the radical critique of the modern and the cultural shift – are not utterly isolated from each other. Break-up, destabilization, anti-modernism, multiple frameworks of meaning, play and polemics are themes that occur in both the interpretive orientation and the social descriptions of the postmodern turn.

What is beauty's fate in the postmodern turn – that is, in a culture marked by iconoclasms towards all past traditions, pervasive marketing, narcissistic orientations and multiple identities? Because contemporary society is only partially receptive to the postmodern, it may be that beauty (as a deep value, a discourse and a way of interpreting and experiencing the world) still survives in nostalgic, antiquarian and traditionalist strands of culture. But in society's most powerful institutions, dominant discourses and cultural 'tones', beauty seems to be very much the beast.

The suppression or marginalization of beauty in human societies is certainly not simply a postmodern phenomenon. It comes with virtually all ancient and modern oppressions such as slavery, ghetto isolation, serfdom, peonage and classism. Because an impoverished and marginalized life makes it is very difficult for the slave, the poor or the disenfranchised to develop aesthetic sensibilities, beauty as a culturally accessible value tends to become the possession of the citizen, the nobility, the gentry and the educated classes. With the Industrial Revolution came not only a democratization of education and a blurring of older lines of wealth and privilege, but also factories, wide economic swings, urban concentrations, new locations of wealth and consumerism that brought about aesthetic impoverishment for the worker and even for the new middle class. It was precisely this beauty-less social environment that evoked the protests of the Romantics.[18]

The postmodern turn brought with it new forms of cultural alienation from beauty. Postmodern societies are, of course, industrialized societies insofar as they still depend on the products of various industries. However, their 'cultural tone' and quality of life are no longer dominated by factories but by massive bureaucratic institutions that market, record, and distribute information, entertainment, food, travel, education, religion, war, government and health. The typical environment of those who work is not the factory but either an office or a specific service delivery location (the small speciality shop, the fast food restaurant). These environments on which the postmodern population depends for income almost all survive by marketing. The most visible, utilized and valued entities of the post-industrial society are the car (and other means of transport), places and sources of entertainment (television, sports stadiums), locales of purchasing (shopping centres, mail-order catalogues) and the popular arts. Postmoderns have become accustomed to their waking hours being filled with the aggressive visual and audio marketing of these valued entities, a marketing which is the cultural air the postmodern human being breathes. Further, these valued entities and their marketing spill over into and set the tones and agendas that deliver society's humanizing and artistic values: family, religion, education and the 'high arts'.

So far, this description has been formal and abstract, concerned with general classes of things such as institutions, sports or entertainment. Although their pre-eminence, their function as society's most serious preoccupations, is central and pervasive, these things in themselves do not constitute the postmodern. Less formal is the observation that these valued entities and their marketing are relatively empty of content, that 'the medium is the message'. At this point, the other sense of postmodernism – a certain epistemological and even global orientation – is pertinent. For the epistemological orientation of play, difference, anti-foundation, non-reference, non-system, multiple frames of meaning and identity are not just phenomena of elitist academic fields, literary and artistic criticism, or the 'high arts'. They are very much part of the soap opera, the sit-com, the politician's 'spin', the media's pseudo-events,[19] the lyrics of rock and rap, the therapist's agenda and the policies of international corporations. Ironically, and this is the deepest paradox of the postmodern, that which apparently liberates from the old hegemonies, re-forms as a new, powerful hegemony of all-pervasive marketing pitches.

To be part of such a culture, to grow up in it, work in it for a living, marry and raise children, or live as a single person or parent is inevitably to be pressed towards certain sensibilities and emptied of others. A kind of de-sensitization takes place when the person must respond, even at subliminal levels, minute-by-minute to reality-indifferent sales pitches. Certain primary values and entities (consumerism, sports and entertainments) are reinforced. Also reinforced is the discontented relativism, violence and superficial silliness which is their message. Described here is what Christopher Lasch calls the culture of narcissism. Precisely because it is preoccupied with the immediacies of emotional stimulation (for instance, the escalating demand for salaciousness in the media and the need for countless TNT explosions to assist the movie plot), the narcissistic society promotes a low sensibility to such values as the mystery and unmanipulability of the human other and the integrity and non-utility of nature or animals.[20]

These twentieth-century descriptions of postmodern culture help us understand why or to what extent beauty has such a low status for postmodern institutions, why the postmodern *episteme* and institutions effect a low sensibility to beauty. Already marginalized in the institutions of the Industrial Revolution, beauty is largely absent from the 'contentless' self-promotions and self-understandings of the new bureaucracies and their marketing machines.[21] Perhaps I exaggerate when I say that, for the postmodern, beauty is the beast. To be the beast, beauty must at least be noticed in order to be feared or refuted. In postmodern societies beauty may not have completely disappeared from language, but it is not a self-evident and important value by which postmoderns understand, experience or interpret their world. The marginalization of beauty in postmodern societies is, as we would expect, part of a larger story, the trivialization of everyday life by the near loss of many 'deep symbols' or cultural values such as the 'real', the holy, tradition, nature, obligation and law.[22] Beauty as a deep value has little function in society's principal institutions, perhaps because, to employ Lyotard's thesis, beauty's function depends on being part of a 'master narrative' that society takes for granted.[23] Since the loss of any and all master narratives is a feature of the postmodern, that loss would carry with it a decline of beauty. To say that the tone of postmodern life is determined largely by consumer-related activities which themselves are incompatible with beauty may be another way of describing the loss of a master narrative.

Beauty as the Beast in Christian Traditions

We do not hear any loud complaints about the absence of beauty in postmodern culture from Christian Churches, but we do hear them deplore the absence of prayer in state schools, the decline of public morals, the increase in the number of abortions, the high illegitimate birthrate and the decline of family values. The concept of 'morality', at least of a certain type, seems to be alive and well in contemporary popular religion. From the religious left we hear passionate assaults on sexism, racism, classism and other bigotries. But the decline or absence of beauty in the wider culture is not something which exercises Christian communities of faith. And, insofar as these communities are inevitably part of the ethos and tendencies of their cultural period, this indifference to beauty should not surprise us.

There might, however, be deeper reasons for this silence, this ecclesiastical indifference to beauty's postmodern marginalization. From the outset, beauty has never held a very firm position in the Christian movement. Although, as stated before, our topic is beauty and its relation to faith, not the arts and 'religion and the arts', if we are to understand beauty's presence or absence in the long history of the Christian movement, we cannot simply ignore the arts. All religious faiths including archaic, tribal and non-textual religions make use of the arts, and Christianity is no exception. By way of poetic, visual and musical arts, beauty has always been an intrinsic part of Christian liturgy and celebratory festivals. Early Christianity employed visual arts in catacombs, on house church walls and in its basilicas.[24] Strangely beautiful are the Gregorian chants, textual illuminations by Celtic monks and cathedral architecture. And from the poetic beauties of the Hebrew Bible and Greek and Roman rhetoric, a tradition of beautiful language formed the creeds, liturgies and prayers of the Church. Even theology offers the occasional beautiful text. The Christian movement did not turn away from beauty when it created its sacred spaces, copied its manuscripts and composed its official languages.

At the same time Christianity had another side: a dark suspicion of the use of images in the cult, traditions that suppressed the dramatic and comedic arts and, in some cases, worked to destroy the arts of 'false' Christian groups as well as of other religious faiths. These suspicions erupted in the early controversies over icons and in the early Protestant destruction of church sculptures and paintings.[25] The sad inconoclasm of the Christian destruction of the art treasures of whole cultures – those of the Incas, for instance – is part of the story. In addition, some forms of Protestantism opposed the arts (novels, dances, theatre) for encouraging idleness and immorality.[26] So beauty does reside in the Christian past through the arts, but its status is always shaky and problematic. In the sphere of the arts there have been times and places when the Christian movement treated beauty as the beast.

This ambivalence in the sphere of the arts becomes a virtual absence when we look for the theme of beauty in Christian piety – that is, how Christians actually conceive and talk about what it is to be Christian, to have faith and to live a redemptively transformed existence. That may be what is behind another of Simone Weil's passionate outbursts:

> ... in general making suitable reservations for the treasures that are unknown, little known, or perhaps buried among the forgotten ruins of the Middle Ages, we might say that the beauty of the world is almost absent from the Christian tradition.[27]

Is this true? The issue here is not iconoclasm – whether the holy is representable, whether pictures should hang in churches – nor is it the moral issue whether Christians should patronize secular theatres. The issue is what is meant by faith itself – the nature and content of faith in God, and the character of a life transformed by grace. We do find in classical Catholic theology occasional revivals of the Hellenic motif of divine beauty. We also find occasional mention of the Platonic notion of the beauty of human virtue. John Bunyan's 'Christian' does discover a 'stately palace', which is beautiful because it houses certain virtues. But when we closely consult the standard expressions of piety in the prayers, liturgies, sermons, journals and letters of the ages, we find beauty to be largely absent. It is not in Coleridge's 'spiritual religion'. It is not a recurrent theme in Puritan, Methodist, Reformed, Lutheran or Anglican pieties nor in their casuistries of positive and negative practices. Nor is beauty anywhere to be found in contemporary exhortations to praxis, social liberation and world change. For the most part, in Christian piety, beauty is the beast, something to be excluded, marginalized or ignored.

How does *theology* fare in the matter? Does theology, that centuries-long effort to interpret faith, Gospel, God and the Christian life, restore what piety lacks? It seems not. Again, there are always exceptions, notably Jonathan Edwards, Hans Ur Von Balthasar and the occasional Thomist and Whiteheadian theologian, but, on the whole, beauty is a rarity in 2000 years of the Christian interpretation of the Gospel. Of course, 'theology' is now a term with multiple meanings, references, types and approaches. All the types (historical, practical, philosophical, systematic) and approaches (neo-Reformation, apologetic, feminist, African-American, liberationist, correlational) share at least one thing in common, a disinterest in beauty. Historical theology has rarely, if ever, conducted inquiries into the thematic of beauty in major or minor historical periods, religious traditions (Catholic, Protestant) or major figures.[28] Historical theology's disinterest no doubt reflects beauty's low profile in the periods, branches or figures themselves. Systematic theologies, both ancient and modern, have not needed the theme of beauty in order to articulate the *loci* of doctrine, construct explanatory systems, relate Christian doctrine to problems of truth, meaning and relevance, or understand the practical dimension of Christian faith and Gospel. A philosophical theology, as we would expect, is receptive to beauty only insofar as beauty is a constituent of the specific philosophy that serves as its framework. Hence, it is almost totally absent in analytic philosophy of religion, it is present to a small degree in Thomist theologies, and is seriously attended to in at least some Whiteheadian theologies. Practical theology has undergone many shifts of meaning and self-understanding in recent decades, but whether it is a term for ministry studies, studies of praxis, or studies of the life of the Church in the world, we do not find it preoccupied with beauty. In the various contemporary theological movements or schools, beauty's absence prevails. It does not even play a minor role in Protestant conservative, neo-Reformation confessional, hermeneutic, correlational, or deconstructive and post-structural theologies. Nor do we find it in what may be the most globally widespread theological movement of the late twentieth century, the praxis or political theologies of liberation: African-American, womanist, South American, Minjung, radical feminist and Asian.

Hebraic and Christian Iconoclasms

Beauty has never obtained the status of a central metaphor in the self-understanding of the major branches of the Christian movement throughout the centuries. It survived from Hellenic times as a relatively minor element in Catholic theologies of God but had virtually no presence in Reformation theologies. If this is the case, the Protestant movement appears to be, at least in relation to beauty, a new and severe iconoclasm that suppresses aesthetic elements in the interpretation of faith.[29] In the face of this aesthetic sparseness throughout Christian history, we are prompted to ask for an explanation. How could beauty have such a low status in such a faith as Christianity, especially its Protestant form? What happened in the history of the Christian faith, a faith that could produce a Dante, a Hildegard of Bingen, a Coleridge or an Emerson, to make possible the following event described by Samuel Leuchli.[30] Leuchli asked a Swiss lay preacher visiting Chicago if he planned to visit the art museum. Leuchli records the reply. ' "Beautiful?" the man repeated incredulously. "Art museum?" He made a fist toward me: "I preach nothing but Jesus Christ crucified," he exclaimed.'

I have already suggested that broad historical forces of industrialization tend to expel beauty from postmodern institutions, and this cannot but affect the Christian movement. Frank Burch Brown traces the cultural decline of beauty to the Renaissance and the historical trend towards secularization. The outcome was 'aesthetic purism' – that is, the insistence that the aesthetic must be utterly independent of any and all religion, and must occupy a secular realm that religion itself can do without.[31] Perhaps so. But in addition to this external explanation, we also should enquire whether historical Christianity contains a powerful and intrinsic anti-aesthetic, a strand that urges believers to think of beauty as the beast. I cannot develop this theme in a definitive or even adequate way, but I can suggest what appear to be certain tendencies in the long and ever variable history of Christianity that work to suppress beauty. Three tendencies especially come to mind: the monotheistic revolution and its ensuing iconoclasms; otherworldliness and moral asceticism; and apocalypticism.

One significant strand of the Christian movement's historical background is the iconoclasm that characterized the ancient Semitic, 'monotheistic' revolution against archaic nature religions.[32] This revolution mounted a severe assault on ancient ways of experiencing the sacred as a set of immanent powers dispersed throughout nature – powers that made things grow and heavenly bodies move, powers that presided over fertility, birth, and death, love and war. From the perspective of Hebraism's radical monotheism, the sacred powers of Canaan, Babylonia and Egypt were powerless idols. The issue at stake was not whether reason prompts us to think of the sacred as single or plural. Rather, the monotheistic turn of Hebraic religion was an ethical rigorism, a summons to moral obedience to the one God who would hold history's peoples accountable to canons of justice. It was justice that prompted the Hebrews to think of deity as a single, personal law-giver rather than as a distributed set of powers of storm, wave, sun and mountain.

One thing seems clear about the archaic, tribal types of faith. The sacred was understood as something at work in the very flow of the universe, in the world's particular capacities to empower, beautify, or even destroy.[33] And because sacred powers are dangerous, any dealing with them called for a complex system of taboos. By way of taboo and ritual, the tribe or clan was attuned to the power and beauty of virtually everything in both the immediate locale and in the cosmos. It is no accident that these faiths engendered arts that produced stunningly beautiful artefacts. With the monotheistic revolution comes a very different relation to the world. If the gods of mountains, waters and fertility are idols, even demons as Paul says, the many taboos are replaced with one great taboo – a terror of idolatry so powerful that it empties all the particulars and regions of the world of their mysterious sacral dimension.

For most faiths (religions), the world's very coming into being, in meadow and glade, in animal life and starry sky, is itself a manifestation of immanent divine powers. To be related to the world's particulars is also to be related to the divine powers at work in them. Whether the particulars are a differentiated order (the fascination of classical Olympian religion) or are an outcome of powers of fertility (the fascination of archaic religions), they are attractive, yet threatening and grotesque. Thus when polytheistic religions express the sacred in song, dance, figurine, sculpture and mask, they express the playful, perilous symmetries and asymmetries of the world. Beautification is not the

only work of the gods, but it is one part of their work as the world is infused
with fertility, order, symmetry, differentiation and power.

Radical monotheism, initially prompted by suspicions of the identification
of divine power with corrupt monarchies and human systems, engenders a
comprehensive suspension of all god–world identities, all immanent distri-
butions of the sacred throughout nature and the human world. This shatters
the ancient correlations between immanent deities and the harmonies and
fertilities of the world. The immanent deities are 'false gods', and the determination to eradicate them carries with it deep suspicions of their immanent
work of beautification.

If the Torah and the Torah-based covenant that constantly confronts the
morally corrupted society is the epiphany of the true God, then the beauty that
attends nature's birth must be the epiphany of the false gods. If the gods and
goddesses make nature shimmer with beauty, then to eradicate them affects a
people's relation to nature. Certainly, in the monotheistic revolution, nature is
created by God, but this creation is not so much a teasing of chaos into splendid
symmetries as a differentiation of realms and types of being by way of a single
primordial act of divine freedom. Further, the whole created world is primarily
a scenario for human beings to work out the moral dimension that virtually
defines them and, in the Christian eschatology, their eventual or ultimate destiny
is to leave nature behind. Hence, the monotheistic fascination is less with
nature and its particular beauties as with human beings, the future of the elect
nation or people, and the transnatural realm that is in store for them.

Once nature and the constantly changing universe is emptied of sacred power,
the initial suspicion of nature's beauties and symmetries extends to language
and the representation of deity. Permissible are metaphors and images for the
divine being and action taken from politics (monarchy), personal responsive-
ness (forgiveness, accusation) and psychological traits (anger, disappointment,
affection). The proper location of these metaphors is language; hence, we
have metaphor and story rather than visual representation. This means that a
profound negative theology arises with the monotheistic revolution that would
destroy all visual icons for deity, especially those taken from nature. The divine
is (non) located in infinity, thus assigned to two cognitively inaccessible realms:
the primordial act of creation, and the ultimate event of world consummation.
In the monotheistic revolution, God 'speaks' and 'acts' – in other words,
communicates through mediating messengers, prophets, texts and events.

However, the universal flow of symmetry, colour and creativity is marginal
to these divine mediations. Thus, the iconoclasm that locates divine activity
primarily in language, history and politics tends to suppress beauty in the
processes of nature and to eliminate it as a theme of piety, narrative and
interpretation.

This is not to say that the iconoclastic faiths have completely emptied
themselves of beauty and the arts. Under the shadow of iconoclastic suspicion,
the arts survived in word and song, phylactery and temple, and icons survived
by way of Gregory the Great's didactic rationale that they relate the faith to
the unlearned.[34] With such didacticism came a use of the arts and, with that, a
use of beauty. But even as faith declines when it simply serves a therapeutic,

aesthetic or even moral usage, so beauty declines when it becomes a utility. As didactically and even liturgically used, beauty remains external to piety, to the experience of nature and to the human being's relationship with the world.

Moral asceticism or otherworldliness is a second element at work in Christian tendencies to suppress beauty. Typically, we identify asceticism with its extreme forms, the deliberate subjection of mind and body to punishing self-denials – rigours that reduce or even withhold food, comfort and sexuality. But strains of asceticism – that is, self-denials of pleasurable fulfilments – attend virtually all traditional Christian pieties. The following incident, recorded in what may be England's most famous novel, shows this strain in a somewhat exaggerated form. A clergyman is speaking.

> You are aware that my plan in bringing up these girls is, not to accustom them to habits of luxury and indulgence, but to render them hardy, patient, self-denying. Should any little accidental disappointment of the appetite occur, such as the spoiling of a meal, the under or the over dressing of a dish, the incident ought not to be neutralised by replacing with something more delicate the comfort lost, thus pampering the body ...[35]

If giving the body its needed nourishment is 'pampering', how much more would we pamper if we granted the human being its need for beauty? Here is that strand of the Christian movement that is deeply suspicious of the very thing in which beauty finds its initial mediation – the body and the senses, the whole pleasurable interaction with the world that constitutes life itself. To attribute the genesis of human evil to the body, the senses, physical needs and organically originated desires suppresses both the body's graceful beauty and the beauty of the body's environment. But the body is not the only villain in the centuries-long tale of asceticism. A broader asceticism targets the self as unworthy of esteem, attention and pleasurable experience. Self-fulfilments, self-satisfactions, pleasures, the innocent joys that attend engagements with nature, arts and human beings – joys that come with the preoccupations of 'idleness' – must all be rooted out if the human being is to be an uncompromised servant of God. They are incompatible with true spirituality and with the sanctity that lives only from and for God. These asceticisms of body and self may sound old-fashioned to most modern ears. But they do suggest a strand of the past that stole from piety its aesthetic dimension and contributed to making beauty into the beast.

Futurism, the apocalyptic element of the monotheistic revolution, is a third strand of Christian history behind the suppression of the aesthetic. A religious faith can marginalize beauty not only by its suspicions of the body and self but by the way in which it interprets time – that is, the past, present and future. For instance, an apocalyptic type of faith may so despair of the unsavoury present that it places all good things – God, the kingdom of God, salvation, heaven, moral purity and the just society – in the future. Certain prophetic and apocalyptic texts offer bucolic descriptions of peaceful, prosperous, rural life (for example, Hosea 14:4–7) or poetic accounts of the new city of God with bejewelled foundations and gates (Revelation 21–22). These texts do celebrate beauty, but it is a postponed beauty, available only in the age to come. Israel shall be 'a crown of beauty in the hand of the Lord', says Isaiah (62:3). The holy city that shall come down from God out of heaven has a 'radiance like a rare jewel clear as crystal' (Revelation 21: 10–11). In extreme apocalypticism, Satan rules the non-beautiful present age: the beautiful new Jerusalem comes in the future. Aiding and abetting the apocalyptic postponement of beauty was a juridical way of understanding the conditions of future salvation that placed at the very centre of the Gospel a legal transaction. Potentially beautiful things, the splendour (*doxa*) of God and the new life of redemption, are overwhelmed by metaphors of the court-room, the judge, the saved and unsaved, and the legal imputation of righteous-ness. In these juridical schemes beauty is simply absent as part of the human being's relation to God, nature or other human beings. It is apocalyptically postponed as an element of future salvation.

These three themes of the monotheistic revolution (iconoclasm, asceticism and futurism) describe dimensions of Israelite and Christian piety that defer and suppress beauty. They are constantly at work 'behind the scenes' removing beauty as a primary value from faith's ritual, ethical and theological discourses. Have these powerful historical tendencies actually removed beauty from the life of faith? This is the question we must now address.

Notes

1 Hans Urs von Balthasar, *The Glory of the Lord: A Theological Aesthetics*, trans. E. Leiva-Merikasis (San Francisco: Ignatius Press, 1983), p. 18.

2 R.S. Thomas, 'The Minister', *Poems of R.S. Thomas* (Fayetteville, Ark: The University of Arkansas Press, 1985), p. 20.

3 For the decline of the motif of beauty in aesthetics and in the arts, see Monroe Beardsly, 'Beauty Since the Nineteenth Century', in Philip Wiener (ed.), *Dictionary of the History of Ideas* (New York: Scribner's, 1968), s. 1.; Patrick Sherry, *Spirit and Beauty: An Introduction to Theological Aesthetics* (Oxford: Clarendon Press, 1992), pp. 24–27. James W. Manns, *Aesthetics* (London: M.E. Sharpe), p. 139ff. Hugo A. Meynell does not see beauty as a suitable term for general aesthetic commendation, although he retains it as one among a number of 'values' that constitute 'aesthetic satisfaction': *The Nature of Aesthetic Value* (Albany, NY: SUNY, 1986), p. 45. For a dismissal of beauty as an older, essentialist (cf. Kant) now discredited theme, see Gordon Graham, *Philosophy of the Arts: An Introduction to Aesthetics* (London: Routledge, 1997). On the banishing of beauty from the humanities, see Elaine Scary, *On Beauty and Being Just* (Princeton, NJ: Princeton University Press, 1999), p. 57.

4 Michel Foucault, *The Archaeology of Knowledge*, trans. A.M.S. Smith (London: Tavistock, 1972), p. 191.

5 Von Balthasar, *The Glory of the Lord*, p. 18.

6 Simone Weil, *Waiting for God* (New York: Putnam, 1951), p. 162.

7 Beauty very much defined the arts in nineteenth-century European romanticism and idealism. Typical is Benedetto Croce's words, 'What good is all the flurry of the passion if the Spirit does not end up with a beautiful image?': *Guide to Aesthetics*, trans. P. Romanell (South Bend, Ind.: Regnery/Gateway, 1965), p. 24. See also Friedrich Schiller, 'Letters on the Aesthetic Education of Man', in *Essays*, trans. W. Hinderer and D.O. Dahlstrom (New York: Continuum, 1993), especially Letters 15 and 16; K.W.F. Schlegel, 'The Limits of

the Beautiful,' in *The Aesthetic and Miscellaneous Works of Friedrich Schlegel*, trans. E.J. Millington (London: H.G. Bohn, 1849); G.W.F. Hegel, 'Introduction', *Aesthetics: Lectures in Fine Art*, trans. T.M. Knox (Oxford: Clarendon Press, 1975). Friedrich Schelling maintained that beauty expresses the *ideal* side of art (in contrast to the 'real' side): *The Philosophy of Art*, trans. D.W. Stott (Minn.: University of Minnesota Press. 1989), #65. For a survey of eighteenth- and nineteenth-century authors who made beauty the centre and definition of the arts, see Leo N. Tolstoy, *What is Art?*, trans. A. Maude (Indianapolis: Library of Liberal Arts, 1960), Chapter 3.

8   Marshall Berman argues that, because one of the features of the modern is an anti-modern resistance to the modern's capacity to destroy values and communities through massive bureaucracies, the modern has a nostalgic element: 'Introduction', *All That is Solid Melts into Air: The Experience of Modernity* (New York: Simon and Schuster, 1982).

9   Oscar Wilde, 'The Burden of Itys', from *The Poems and Fairy Tales of Oscar Wilde* (New York: Modern Library, 1932), p. 102.

10   On the multiple meanings of postmodernism, see Charles Jencks, *What is Postmodernism?* (New York: St Martin's Press, 1987), Chapter II; David R. Griffin, 'Introduction', *Founders of Postmodern Philosophy* (Albany, New York: SUNY, 1993). Richard Bernstein argues that the very terminology and distinction between the modern and the postmodern has become philosophically unfruitful: *The New Constellation: The Ethico-Political Horizon of Modernity/Postmodernity* (Cambridge, MA: MIT Press, 1992), p. 200, and Introduction.

11   For modernity and modernism, see Berman, *All That is Solid Melts into Air*, Introduction; Robert Neville, *The High Road Around Modernism* (Albany, NY: SUNY, 1992), Introduction, II; Jürgen Habermas, *The Philosophical Discourse of Modernism* (Cambridge: Polity Press, 1988); Lawrence E. Cahoone, *The Dilemma of Modernity: Philosophy, Culture, and Anti-Culture* (Albany, NY: SUNY, 1988), pp. 2–8.

12   According to Steven Best and Douglas Kellner, parody, critique, subversion and demystification are part of the two sides of the postmodern, the other being the playful: *The Postmodern Turn* (New York: Guilford Press, 1997), Chapter 4.

13   Richard Kearney describes these themes in the phrase, 'aesthetic undecidability', in which the creative, ethical project of human culture gives way to the 'demise of the imagination' and even truth itself: *The Wake of the Imagination: Toward a Postmodern Culture* (Minn.: University of Minnesota Press, 1988).

14   Some of the primary interpreters of this cultural shift follow. Frederic Jameson, *The Postmodern Turn: Essays in Postmodern Theory and Culture* (Durham, NC: Duke University Press, 1991); Jean-François Lyotard, *The Postmodern Condition: A Report on Knowledge*, trans. Bennington and Massumi (Minn.: University of Minnesota Press, 1984); Kenneth Gergen, *The Saturated Self: Dilemmas of Identity in Contemporary Life* (New York: Basic Books, 1991); Philip Rieff, *The Feeling Intellect: Selected Writings* (Chicago: University of Chicago Press, 1990); Daniel Boorstin, *The Image: A Guide to Pseudo Events in America* (New York: Atheneum, 1987); Christopher Lasch, *The Culture of Narcissism: American Life in an Age of Diminished Expectations* (New York: Norton, 1978); Marshal Berman, *op. cit.*; Charles Jencks, *What is Postmodernism?*

15   On the aesthetic impoverishment brought about by a consumer society that reduces the arts to consumer cultural objects and entertainments, see Hannah Arendt, 'The Crisis in Culture', in *Between Past and Future: Exercises in Political Thought* (New York: Viking Press, 1968).

16   Poston calls it 'an aesthetic new world'.

17   Christopher Lasch, *The Culture of Narcissism: American Life in an Age of Diminished Expectations* (New York: Norton, 1978).

18   'Spirit of Beauty, tarry yet awhile!
Although the cheating merchants of the mart
With iron roads profane our lovely isle,
And break on whirling wheels the limbs of art,'
(Oscar Wilde, 'The Garden of Eros', *The Poems and Fairy Tales of Oscar Wilde*, p. 64.)

19   Daniel J. Boorstin, *The Image: A Guide to Pseudo Events in America* (NY: Atheneum, 1987).

20   For an account of how modern culture gave rise to a new 'dehumanized art', see Ortega
     y Gasset, *On the Dehumanization of Art and Other Essays in Art, Culture, and Literature*
     (Princeton, NJ: Princeton University Press, 1968).
21   George Steiner has discovered how academia is itself a sprawling bureaucracy that promotes
     an anti-aesthetic through a massive machine of commentary and secondary discourse that
     displaces 'real presences' and the immediacy of things, even texts, themselves: *Real
     Presences* (Chicago: University of Chicago Press, 1989), pp. 24–47.
22   See the author's *Deep Symbols: Their Postmodern Effacement and Reclamation* (Valley
     Forge, PA: Trinity Press, 1996). The concept of 'deep symbol' is discussed in Chapter 1.
23   See Lyotard, *op. cit.*, *The Postmodern Condition*, Chapter 10.
24   For art (and beauty) in the early period of the Christian movement, see Walter Lowrie, *Art
     in the Early Church* (New York: Harper and Row, 1965); Samuel Leuchli, *Religion and
     Art in Conflict: Introduction to a Cross-disciplinary Task* (Philadelphia: Fortress Press,
     1980), Chapter 6; John Dillenberger, *A Theology of Artistic Sensibilities: The Visual Arts
     and the Church* (New York: Crossroads, 1986), Chapter 1; Pierre du Bourquet, *Early
     Christian Painting*, trans. S.W. Taylor (London: Weidenfeld and Nicolson, 1966); and
     Sherry, *Spirit and Beauty*, pp. 4–12.
25   On the history of Christian iconoclasm and anti-art, see Leuchli, *Religion and Art in Conflict*,
     Chapters 1–6, and Gerardus van der Leeuw, *Sacred and Profane Beauty: The Holy in Art*,
     trans. David E. Green (New York: Holt, Rinehart, and Winston, 1963), the third chapters
     of each of the four Parts of the work.
26   On early Protestant suppressions of art, see Mortimer Adler, *Art and Prudence: A Study in
     Practical Philosophy* (New York: Longmans Green and Co., 1937), Chapter 3.
27   Simone Weil, *Waiting for God*, p. 161.
28   The exception is that Thomas Aquinas (and the Middle Ages) and Jonathan Edwards have
     both evoked a few works on beauty in their thought. On Aquinas, see Umberto Eco, *The
     Aesthetics of Thomas Aquinas*, trans. H. Bradin (Cambridge, MA: Harvard University
     Press, 1988), and *Art and Beauty in the Middle Ages*, trans. H. Bradin (New Haven, CT:
     Yale University Press, 1986). On Edwards see Roland Delattre, *Beauty and Sensibility in
     the Thought of Jonathan Edwards: An Essay in Aesthetics and Theological Ethics* (New
     Haven, CT: Yale University Press, 1968); and Terrence Erdt, *Jonathan Edwards: Art and
     the Sense of the Heart* (Amherst, MA: University of Massachusetts Press, 1980).
29   On the iconoclastic element of the Reformation and the Protestant movement, see
     Dillenberger, *A Theology of Artistic Sensibilities*, Chapters 3 and 4. See also G.G. Coulton,
     Art and the Reformation (Cambridge: Cambridge University Press, 1953), Chapter XX.
30   Samuel Leuchli, *op.cit.*, Preface.
31   Frank Burch Brown, *Religious Aesthetics: A Theological Study of Making and Meaning*
     (Princeton, NJ: Princeton University Press, 1989), pp. 5–6, 47–50.
32   On the iconoclasm of Israel and Judaism, see Joseph Gutman, 'The Second Commandment
     and the Image of Judaism', *Hebrew Union College Annual*, (32), 1961, pp. 161–74. Gutman
     contends that the forbidding of images was meant to assure loyalty to the invisible Yahweh
     and expresses the opposition of nomadic, tribal cultures to the idols of sedentary peoples.
     See also Richard Viladesau, *Theological Aesthetics: God in Imagination, Beauty, and Art*
     (New York: Oxford University Press, 1999), pp. 184–85. On the beauty of the Jewish
     tradition, see John T. Petuchowski, 'The Beauty of God', in Joseph A. Edelheit (ed.), *The
     Life of the Covenant: The Challenge of Contemporary Judaism. Essays in Honor of Herman
     E. Schaalman* (Chicago: Spertus College of Judaica Press, 1986).
33   On aesthetics and the arts (especially dance) in archaic cultures, see van der Leeuw, *Sacred
     and Profane Beauty*, Part One, p. 1. See also Mircea Eliade, *Symbolism, the Sacred and
     the Arts*, ed. D. Apostolos-Cappadona (New York: Crossroads, 1985).
34   Brown, *op.cit.*, *Religious Aesthetics*, Introduction.
35   Charlotte Bronte, *Jane Eyre* (New York: Modern Library, 1847), p. 65.

Chapter 2

Beauty as Being: The Irrepressible Character of Beauty

So beauty on the waters stood
When love had severed earth from flood!
So when he parted air from fire,
He did with concord all inspire. (Ben Jonson)[1]

An actual fact is a fact of aesthetic experience (Alfred North Whitehead)[2]

Chapter 1 told the rather grey tale of beauty's curtailment in postmodern institutions and in latter-day Christian pieties and theologies. The passing of beauty is a poignant theme for the Romantic poets: 'Where is beauty? Gone, gone' says one of them.[3] Do their laments exaggerate? Has beauty fled postmodern societies and the iconoclastic faiths? All statements about real things call for qualifications and supplementations. Industrial and postmodern societies, and Christian pieties and theologies, have not eliminated beauty from human experience or religious communities, although cultural, religious and theological suppressions of beauty may cause postmoderns to overlook it. Yet, the past has a way of countering this cultural loss of memory. Beautiful works from former times are still with us. Many great buildings, sculptures, picturesque villages, musical works and works of literature can still be seen, heard and read. The physical and cultural world in which we live is furnished and shaped by these survivals. If these furnishings were to disappear, our lives would not simply be impoverished, they would not 'be' at all. Many postmoderns have to struggle not to downgrade the survivals of past beauty to mere quaintness. And we must acknowledge that medieval Marian cathedrals (such as Chartres), Elizabethan dramas and Celtic illuminated manuscript suggest worlds that nowadays elude us.

A second reason to qualify claims that beauty has disappeared is the fact that, here at the beginning of a new millennium, artists, musicians, painters, landscapers, poets, craftspeople, potters and dancers still work their magic. And despite what seems to be a determination by some of them to transcend, or even abolish, the orientations to beauty, we still experience a certain beauty even in their attempts to reveal the sordid, the chaotic, and the dull. The relationship between the arts and beauty – always a disputed matter – continues to recede as an important aesthetic issue. At this point we can concede the rather obvious point that any specific work of art contains aims and contents that the notion of beauty does not capture. Something else besides beauty – especially in its classical sense of harmony and unity in variety – may guide an artist's projects. Whether the artist can pursue these larger aims and, at the same time, be utterly indifferent to beauty is the issue. And this turns us toward the question of the meaning of beauty, and to the subject of this chapter – beauty as being. Even in the artist's most determined attempts at iconoclastic shattering, transcending structure and creative playfulness, it seems that beauty will emerge. If the thesis of this chapter holds, traces of beauty will call to us in the creativity of the artist simply because beauty is 'being'.

In addition to the cultural artefacts of past beauty and traces of beauty in current artistic creativity, another beauty persists from the past – namely the inescapable environs of embodied life. Whatever our culture, and however little we pay attention to or value nature, we never wholly suppress or escape earth, sky, land, forests and seasons: 'the smell of tansy through the dark', as one poet puts it.[4] Thus old and new pastoral poets of nature (John Clare, Wendell Berry) did not so much grieve over something totally lost as recall to mind what is always there. When we try to imagine a nature-less existence, we soon realize how much the quality of life is bound up with an endless succession of everyday beauty that we take for granted.

I conclude, then, that the dismissal of beauty as a quaint, 'romantic' or mistaken notion is premature. There is still too much beauty about us to permit an absolute suppression. The engagements of everyday life with past cultural creations, with contemporary arts and with the overwhelming sights and sounds of nature can never be utterly bereft of aesthetic elements. To understand why this is so, I shall consult a textual legacy of the classical past that claims that beauty comes with being itself.

It is one thing to say that beauty is a feature, however linguistically quaint and out-of-date, of human experience and human culture. It is another to say that beauty is 'being'. I must acknowledge at the outset that twentieth-century philosophies (empiricist, pragmatist, deconstructive) find little use for the term 'being' in their work. They resist the kind of 'essentialist', 'universalizing' or ahistorical thinking for which being is a problem. Like beauty, being is also out of favour. I use the term 'being' as a kind of code word for any referent of thinking that is not a specific object, accidental trait or statistical generalization. To discern human beings not just as amalgams of objective features (such as hair colour, weight and food preferences) but in their distinctive temporality is to address their very 'being'. Again, I must acknowledge that some twentieth-century philosophies eschew 'being' as a usable or meaningful term because they identify it with ancient, or at least premodern (and therefore discredited), cosmologies and metaphysics. Being is the world as distributed into the four elements, as divinely participated, as structured by ideas (*eidoi*), transcendentals, primary qualities and the like, and modern sciences, supposedly, have swept all this away. For others 'being' invites the essentialist and hierarchical thinking complicit in reducing the 'nature' of women, inferior races and various threatening others to types. But the term has the double connotation of what ultimately constitutes the world (cosmos) and of whatever specifically and distinctively is itself. The impulse to interpret being in either sense reveals a bafflement that persists after specific empirical inquiries have been conducted and answered. For Alfred North Whitehead, this impulse is towards philosophy itself.[5] After the data have been gathered about the causes, behaviour and structure, of a particular event or entity – for example, a certain rainforest fungus – the philosopher is still baffled by the mysterious phenomenon of the human act of knowing. And after the various theories about cosmic origins, destinies and structure are presented, the philosopher remains baffled by the very fact of the cosmos and about the way in which its most general features (such as its process and structure) relate to each other.

Although this detour may be too brief to persuade the sceptic that 'being' exists or to make sense of it to those not interested in philosophy, I make it because the consideration of being – that is, questions concerning both the mystery of the creation of the cosmos itself and the 'being' of human being – underlies the long history of Western fascination with beauty. For Western philosophy from its inception through the Middle Ages and for those moderns who remain in touch with those traditions, it has been impossible to isolate beauty from the 'thinking of being'. In what follows I attempt to give an account of the classical, Hellenic philosophy of beauty as it finds its way into the Christian Middle Ages, and the emendation of this tradition in Alfred North Whitehead. Both Platonic and Whiteheadian (process) philosophies restate and confirm the common-sense intuition of everyday life experience that nothing can 'be' without being, in some sense and to some degree, beautiful.

The 'Great Theory of Beauty'

A powerful consensus about beauty prevailed throughout the history of Western culture from early Hellenic times to the eighteenth century. According to Wladyslaw Tartarkiewicz, 'the great theory of the beauty' originated with Pythagoras and gained elaboration in Plato and subsequent Platonists (for example, Plotinus).[6] The great theory is then given Christian reformulation in St Augustine, Pseudo-Dionysius the Areopagite, Anicius Boethius, Duns Scotus Erigena, St Bonaventure and Thomas Aquinas.[7] Proponents of the great theory agree that, whatever beauty itself is, to experience it is pleasurable.[8] For Bonaventure, to grasp any object whatsoever provokes delight, and thus human beings' very experience of the world is pleasurable (*suavitas*).[9] But there are many kind of pleasures. What is it that evokes the distinctive pleasure that arises with experiencing beauty? According to the great theory, it is *proportion* – the harmony of the parts to a whole – that engenders this distinctive pleasure and, because proportion is the explanation, it can be called a 'theory' of beauty. Because nothing can have actual existence without some proportion. Every response to some degree has a pleasurable element.

The Olympian Cosmogonies

Where does the great theory come from? For Tartarkiewicz, Pythagoras is its creator. For the Pythagoreans the mathematical relations (proportions, harmonies) of musical sounds stimulate pleasure in music. A line from Samuel Taylor Coleridge succinctly expresses this theory: 'And what if all of animated

nature be but organic Harps diversely framed that tremble into thought....?'[10]
The Pythagorean accomplishment was to render into mathematical conceptuality a motif – one might even say *the* motif – of pre-classical Hellenic
religion, the cosmogonical theme of the victory of order over chaos. This
theme had already found expression in ancient Near Eastern (Babylonian,
Egyptian and Canaanite) cosmogonies. These cosmogonic traditions and other
cosmic genealogies reappear in what Robert Graves called the Pelasgian
creation myths (Homeric, Orphic) – a tradition that finds systematized
expression in Hesiod's *Theogony*.[11]

Present-day postmoderns are typically fascinated with the phenomena of
difference, change, chaos and destabilization. Heraclitus, the prophet of change,
not Plato, is our ancient hero. By contrast, the Hellenic fascination was with
the astonishing fact that there is a world at all. How could there be such a
vibrant, living, unified, multilayered thing? How could the differentiated
regions of sky, earth, seas and mountains ever come about? And how could
there be such constraints on these titanic, destructive powers that seasons come
and go, the sun and planets appear on schedule, and living things flood the
planet in a recurring orgy of birth? It all seemed like a sheer miracle. Nor was
this differentiated, ordered world simply an eternal structure, a given fact.
Rather, its orders and regularities took place in an ongoing struggle with
phthora – a passing away. For there to be a world at all, there must be a
continual victory over awesome powers which, if not held in check, would
quickly turn cosmos into chaos. This is the great theme of all the Hellenic
cosmogonies.[12]

Some of these cosmogonies are closer to their mythical roots than others.
But certain themes recur in all of them. First, the Orphic and Hesiod
cosmogonies are at the same time theogonies – accounts of the origins of the
very powers that engender cosmos. And only *divine* powers can tame the mighty
forces of chaos so as to bring about differentiated realms. Second, these are
patriarchal cosmogonies. The White Goddess of pre-Olympian times is there
in the reduced role of consort, muse, grace, earth (gaia), moon, huntress and
corn maiden.[12] Third, the journey from chaos to cosmos is made up of phases,
each one a further step away from chaos towards a new order, which in turn is
the framework and presupposition for the next phase. For instance, in Hesiod's
account of creation, the realms of earth (*gaia*) and sky (*ouranos*) are the
necessary locales of more specific powers and regions such as the ocean, and
time (*kronos*), both born of earth and sky. Fourth, the primary metaphor of
creation is war, conflict and struggle between powers. Creation means over-
coming the resisting powers of chaos – a resistance that artists also face when
they struggle with materials of clay, stone, gravity, larynx or language. And
with each new phase, the chaos element is again encountered, tamed into
order, but never eliminated. Titans, giants, powers of Hades and capricious
chance never simply disappear from the cosmos, and the cosmos is never
simply sheer order but rather an ongoing ordering struggle.[14] Hesiod
systematized the Orphic tradition; Plato's *Timaeus*, an important text for
Christian medieval cosmologies, articulated the dynamism of world ordering.
Fifth, what is it that works to squeeze the cosmos out of chaos and force

stability through phase after phase? Ovid was to say that deity (*deus*) brought sky, earth and the rest out of the 'warring seeds'.[15] In Ovid's account, the gods and goddesses come later with the Golden Age. But for Hesiod, the great cosmologist of the Homeric age, it was Eros that generated gods and cosmos,[16] and this surely was an Olympian and patriarchal replacement for the fecund, generative, ancient goddess. Sixth, the one great opposition in these cosmogonies is between chaos (and its various meanings of empty space, *agon* or strife, warring seeds, unformed potency, passing away) and cosmos, the ordered realm of particular things, each of which is a unity of parts located in its proper region of ocean, river, sky or earth, all moving through time and overshadowed by celestial regularity. To be, then, means to emerge out of chaos, to provisionally hold chaos at bay, to possess at least a minimum of order, stability and harmony. Finally, Hesiod describes Eros as *kallistos*, the most beautiful of the gods. Thus, the generative power of being is itself beautiful. Why? Because beauty is the very thing Eros brings about – an order in struggle with chaos.[17] Such was the legacy of the Olympian cosmogonies already in place prior to the philosophical formulations of the great theory in Pythagoras, the Stoics, Plato, Plotinus, St Augustine and the theologies of the Christian Middle Ages. In these cosmogonies it was simply self-evident that to be meant to be ordered and harmonious, and to be harmonious was to be beautiful.

The Platonic Tradition

The Hellenic demythologizing of the Olympian cosmogonies in Ionian science, Stoic and Epicurean cosmologies, and in Plato and Aristotle, is the event or movement in which Western philosophy had its origin. Here the great theory of beauty obtains its initial conceptual articulation. In Plato's *Philebus*, Hesiod's cosmogony seems to be put aside.[18] The dialogue takes up the question of the proper object of desire (*epithumia*) and proceeds to argue that this object can only be whatever is the best and highest. The entities of the visible world with the satisfactions they bring cannot be the *highest* objects of desire. Genuine desire would press on to whatever is the highest and best – namely, to whatever is truly real. At this point Plato uses the term *eros* for this desire and, suddenly, we are called back to Hesiod. Like beautiful Eros that generates the cosmos, there is also a hungry and thirsty *eros* of the soul that can be satisfied only by whatever is the highest – that is, what constitutes the very reality of the cosmos. And this reality cannot be merely the ephemeral passing away of things which the senses perceive, because something besides mere passing makes possible the naissance and persistence of things; something constitutes the power and content of each thing as grasped by genuine knowledge (*episteme*), or wisdom (*sophia*). And that enduring, constitutive power that makes any and all things real is the constitutive and distinctive form of things, the defining reality of human beings, earth, justice and education.

Now, a Pythagorean interpretation of Plato (which in fact has tended to prevail through the centuries) would say that by form (*eidos*) Plato means structure, pattern and number. An alternative interpretation contends that the form (what true knowledge apprehends as distinctive) is not merely a thing's static structure but its power and way of being. In this interpretation Plato's demythologizing of Hesiod becomes more apparent. For what are the gods and goddesses of each phase of creation but the ordering *powers* of the differentiated realms of the cosmos? When these personalized deities are demythologized, they become the distinctive forms that true knowledge apprehends. To apprehend these forms, says Plato, is to grasp something that is *kalos*, beautiful. And, with this step, the Olympian mytho-poetic tradition finds philosophical expression. Here, too, *to be* is to be beautiful, but being is a complex of differentiated forms ordered under something that transcends all form, which is itself never an object of knowledge – namely, the Good.

Well into the Christian era (the third century), Plotinus continues the Platonic tradition's fascination with beauty.[19] In one passage he appears to depart from the great theory, criticizing the notion that beauty is itself simply the quantitative symmetry of parts in relation. If this is what beauty is, there is no way to account for why a partless phenomenon, such as colour, the sunlight or a flash of lightning, is beautiful. Since a symmetrical face can also be ugly, something else is at work in a beautiful face than mere symmetry. He further argues that an external symmetry of parts in relation does not show how virtue (*areté*) is beautiful.[20] These criticisms do constitute a departure from Pythagorean and certain Stoic versions of the great theory. The Plotinian departure is launched by a refusal to allow the distinction between form and matter to determine the question, the result being that beauty falls on the side of ordered patterns in contrast to chaos, matter or body. For Plotinus the divine realm is neither a mere abstract unity (the One) nor the One manifested in the intelligible order (*nous*). It is also the animating power of things, a livingness surging through the universe (*psuché*). Accordingly, human participation in the divine is not merely an openness to intelligibility – the realm of the *eidoi* or forms – by way of knowledge but is also vitality or soul (*psuché*). True, to express beauty objectively, Plotinus sees the intelligible world as beauty's primary location; thus the *eidoi*, the true forms of things, make all actual things beautiful. But apart from the soul and its desires, and the wisdom that orients the soul towards the forms, nothing is really beautiful. Beauty, in other words, is the intelligibility of things played out or spilt over into the animating power of the world and, specifically, to the animated or ensouled human being. Beauty is not, then, mere order or pattern but is an ensouled or enlivened intelligibility whose origin is the beyond-being or One.

The Great Theory in the Middle Ages

While aesthetics in the Christian Middle Ages has been the subject of extensive historical inquiry, a history of beauty in patristic and medieval periods has yet to be written.[21] And while architecture, sculpture, music and words profoundly shaped medieval Christendom, sometimes giving rise to controversies about the arts (hence the iconoclastic controversy and Bernard's criticisms of the ornate Cluniac churches), medieval Christian thinkers produced no overall theory of the arts. Similarly, the Christian Middle Ages produced no focused, independent and developed theory of beauty. However, a few small tracts and occasional passages are sufficient to show what happened to the great theory of beauty in the 'Christian philosophy' of the Middle Ages.[22] As we would expect, the medieval doctors did not pluck the theme of beauty directly from Plato, Plotinus and Aristotle. Beauty had already found occasional and undeveloped thematization in the Neo-Platonic theologians of the patristic period: for instance, in St Augustine, Pseudo-Dionysius, Boethius and Duns Scotus Erigena.[23] The medieval theologians do appropriate the great theory of beauty but transplant it into a Christian metaphysics. From Plato through Plotinus, the Greek texts were demythologized accounts of the Hellenic theogonies. Thus, beauty as order or symmetry is an ever-present, ever-ongoing victory of divine powers over powers of chaos. In the words of A.H. Armstrong:

> There is no question of the divine belonging to and intervening from a higher or different sphere or world. The gods are born in the world. They do not make it. The starting point for awareness of divine enhancement of the world's beauties is a general awareness of divinity present everywhere and an apprehension of it is all experience.[24]

Beauty is not just ultimate form but a constantly accomplished in-forming of all things as the world as cosmos ever comes about. Plato's *Timaeus* is one of Hellenism's most rigorous expressions of this cosmology, but early Christian polemics against Mediterranean polytheisms replaced this metaphysics of the ongoing divine reduction of chaos to order with the free, sovereign and creative act of God. Beauty continues to be form, symmetry and order but, instead of being distributed into the divinely emanated and multiple realm of forms, it is located eternally in the mind and vision of God. A single primordial act of creation whose outcome was the world system reproduced, in contingent and finite mode, the eternally envisioned forms. In the words of Duns Scotus Erigena, God's beauty 'draws all things to himself [sic]', producing the 'general harmony of the universe itself'.[25] This shift to the analogical beauty of a created world sharply distinguished from the creator resulted in a less dynamic or processional way of understanding beauty. I call this Christian emendation a different 'metaphysic' because it displaces the essentially tragic way of understanding the world as a perpetual and unavoidable struggle between chaos and order.

Despite this shift of metaphysics, beauty was present in the thought of the medieval doctors for the same reason that it was present in the Hellenic thinkers. With the exception of occasional passages on the beauty of virtue – a pre-Christian as well as a Christian theme – the theologians discover beauty as they track the way God creates and disposes the world. Thus, cosmology, and the puzzle of the world, is theology's route to beauty. Beauty does not originate with the onset of faith, Christian ethics, or the drama of sin and redemption. Rather, it enters the halls of theology by way of contemplation of the world's divinely in-formed proportions. Plato and Plotinus thus are much more responsible for the theme of surviving beauty in the Christian texts than biblical texts, Gospel, faith or redemption.

This is not to say that the Christian thinkers were content to depict beauty as simply pattern, the view that Plotinus opposed. First, the theologians, especially Bernard, like Cicero, the Stoics and others, insisted not only that virtues and the heart could be beautiful, but that the primary beauty was inner beauty.[26] Second, the theologians followed Plotinus in saying that beauty is not merely an external feature but something that correlates with a certain kind of experience. Beauty displays itself to a particular human *habitus*, the habit or orientation of intuitive apprehension of pure forms – the knowledge angels have. In the human realm intuitive knowledge takes place in and through the senses. To know through the senses is always a pleasure. Similarly pleasurable is the experience of the beautiful through the senses. Why does beauty evoke pleasure and offer delight to the intellect? The theologians at this point adopt a slightly elaborated version of the great theory. Once Thomas Aquinas locates the experience of beauty in the *habitus* of knowledge, he has the clue to why it is a *delectio*, a pleasure. Human knowing is driven by *desire* for the real and the good. That which can fulfil that desire in contemplative knowledge is either a sense object in-formed by some degree of proportion or a formal object, proportion itself. And if beauty consists of 'due proportion', then any experience of a sense object fulfils a basic desire. Thus to grasp (*spectare*) at all is to experience delight.[28]

There is little question that Aquinas has appropriated the great theory of beauty. All living individuals as they fall into species have the proportion due to their type. Nothing can 'be' without proportion or unity of parts. To fully exist as a thing, a being, is to be so perfected. This means that the thing has obtained sufficient 'integrity' to be itself. Thus, for Aquinas, integrity or perfection is one of the three criteria of beauty. A second criterion is clarity (*claritas*) which is the manifest splendour of proportioned form or entity. Beauty thus is the 'resplendence of form'.[29] We can see now the meaning of Thomas's dictum that beauty is what pleases simply as seen or grasped. To experience anything at all is to experience a pleasing manifest proportion and integrity. To be thus is to be beautiful.

Such was the great theory of beauty as it found its way into the Catholic Christian theologies of the Middle Ages. It did not occupy a central place in theological schemes, obtain an elaborate thematization, nor was beauty employed to interpret the world of faith and redemption. Nevertheless, it offered a way in which Catholic Christianity could attribute beauty both to God and (analogically) to the very being of the world.

Yet, the medieval Christian version of the great theory does leave us with questions – four in particular. First, if *to be* is to be beautiful, why was the theme of beauty withheld from almost every other part of Christian doctrine, morals and piety? The theologians could grant, had to grant, that the virtuous soul is beautiful but they made little of it.

Second, if beauty is the integrity (*perfectio*) of any actualization and its resplendent proportion, nothing can be a body – celestial or terrestrial, or organic, lifeless or living, dangerous or safe – without having at least some beauty. A later text gives powerful expression to this conviction that being is not only good but beautiful: 'I hold there is a general beauty in the works of

God, therefore no deformity in any kind of species or creature whatsoever: I cannot tell by what logic we call a toad, a bear, or an elephant ugly.'[30] Given this conviction that to be is to be beautiful, how do we account for the enormous power of bodily asceticism in Catholic Christianity? Is beauty being suppressed and marginalized even within the metaphysics that affirms its ontological status?

Third, what is the relation between beauty as actualized resplendent proportion and the dynamic, changing flow of things? This question can be addressed to the great theory of beauty in general, not just to the medieval Christian version. To say that beauty is proportion suggests that what makes something beautiful is a fixed structure, that beauty itself is pattern or structure. Plotinus opposed this reduction because it suppressed the animating soul's role in beauty. Robert Bridges agrees: 'This petal'd cap, what is it by the wild fawn's liquid eye / Eloquent as love-music neath the moon.'[31] We have seen that, in the Hellenic cosmogonies, beauty is the ordered outcome of the struggle with chaos; hence it is located in the creative process itself, the constant flow of things into harmony. Thus, beauty always depends on, and even requires, an element of chaos, disorder and pathos: it is a tragic, and not simply triumphal, notion. Is that which is beautiful that great surge of things from an original chaos towards an unknown future, the 'world as a heraclitean fire', as Hopkins says? Or does beauty arise only when things come to rest – a neat pattern hiding in messy matter?

Finally, the mythological, Hellenic, and Christian sources agree that the ultimate source of beauty is God. In some way God imparts beauty to all things. Is God Godself beautiful? If God is, as the scholars say, the eminent instance of all finite perfections, God must be the perfect instance of beauty. But how can this be if beauty means proportion or symmetry? As the One, the utterly Simple Being without parts and complexity, it would seem that God cannot be a unity in difference, for there are no parts to harmonize. And, technically speaking, the persons of the trinity are not parts in a larger whole. How, then, can that which is itself a non-proportion be the archetypal ground of beauty? In classical theism God is an archetypal unity but not unity in variety. This is not unlike the question Christian philosophers and theologians have pressed on the old mythologies. How can chaos, as such, spawn deities, gods and goddesses, the workers of beauty? If chaos is ultimate and primordial, no cosmos will ever arise from it. It can spawn only itself. How, then, does an ultimate Simplicity give rise to the proportioned complexity of beauty? This is the problem that worried Boehme, Schelling and Whitehead.

The Process Transmutation of the Great Theory of Beauty

I have expounded the great theory of beauty in its classical Hellenic and medieval Christian versions. Are we to conclude that in the wake of its eighteenth-century critics, the theory did not survive into modern times? An epitaph on the great theory would be premature. Beauty as proportion survives in Thomist and neo-Thomist aesthetics.[32] However, in addition to those aesthetics that retain the framework of Platonism or Thomism, twentieth-century philosophy saw a restatement of the great theory based on a radically different metaphysics. I speak of Alfred North Whitehead and process philosophy. For process philosophy, too, to be is to be beautiful.

Alfred North Whitehead, the English mathematician and philosopher of science who ended his career at Harvard University, offered up a comprehensive vision that was, for philosophy, not unlike Einstein's vision for physics and cosmology. To discern the basic concepts of that vision sets a task similar to the demands of Einstein's cosmology. Just as to bypass Einstein's mathematics leaves us without the substance of his theory, to bypass Whitehead's conceptual scheme is to blur Whitehead. And this poses a dilemma. Shall I attempt yet another recap of the technical structure of Whitehead's thought or bypass that for a more accessible account? I opt for the second alternative and shall offer a brief and non-technical treatment of the Whiteheadian aesthetic.[33]

Whitehead is one of the few philosophers of modern times whose vision of reality is at the same time a vision of beauty, for whom to be is also to be beautiful.[34] In Whitehead, the main features of the great theory obtain a twentieth-century restatement. Recall the mythical and conceptual elements of the great theory: chaos, strife and battle, eros and teleology, contrast and proportion, perception (*visum*), pleasure and satisfaction, creativity. All these elements are present in Whiteheadian metaphysics. In certain ways Whitehead's account seems closer to Hesiod and the Orphic tradition than to Plato and Plotinus. The reason is that flow, time and creativity, rather than principles, forms, and structures, are at the heart of his understanding of beauty.

Recall one of the unresolved issues of the great theory of beauty. If beauty is proportion but only as experienced as pleasurable to a human subject, where is beauty itself? In the classical Hellenic theory, beauty is located in the objective pattern. For the eighteenth-century critics of that theory, it is in the sensations. Whitehead initially seems to side with the eighteenth century: the location of beauty, the place to look for it, is experience itself. At this point Whitehead presents an extensive, complicated and technical account of experience as a temporal flow made up of moments or occasions. This temporal flow is not so much like a series of houses on a piece of land, each of which is torn down and then replaced, as a tradition that a people inherit, alter slightly and pass on to the next generation. To experience means to receive all sorts of data from the past, such as one's own subconscious traumas, inclinations, biological needs, and explicit memories. But this past surviving information never merely 'causes' or determines experience, because the flow of experience is simultaneously a kind of hunger, a seeking of satisfaction, an orientation to value and disvalue, importance and unimportance.[35] This hunger is at the same time the creative spontaneity of a subject: it is never itself a mere *cause* of experience.

For Whitehead, then, experience is a creative accomplishment, almost a victory. Why is this? First, because the subject of experience is not simply a single agenda or feeling. Multiple states, feelings and moods make up a subject, and these can cancel each other out to the extent that nothing specific is ever experienced. Second, what we receive from the past and perceive in the present is not just a chaotic, meaningless jumble of data. We would never experience a single flower if we were simply subjects of a massive bombardment of a myriad aspects, events, colours, and molecular and cellular data. For perceptive experience to take place at all, both the clash of inner moods (subjective forms in Whitehead's terminology) and perceived data need to be synthesized into some dominant and unified entity. If these syntheses do not take place, there is no perception, experience, realization or knowledge. Experience is in fact the successful accomplishment of these syntheses. In experience the chaos of the world and the chaos of the subject are, at least to a certain degree, resolved. And a pleasure or feeling of satisfaction attends this resolution. To struggle through a maze of meaningless noises or a kaleidoscope of colours in order to hear a melody or perceive a distant mountain carries with it a pleasure. Furthermore, greater complexity, stronger conflicts and more stark incompatibilities set more complex tasks of synthesis or resolution, and result in a greater intensity of feeling and emotion. Beauty, then, is both the harmonious synthesis of oppositions (that is the element from the great theory) and the intense quality of experience that accompanies it.[36] Hence the opposite of beauty is both discord – that is, a chaos or jumble that undermines experience – and the sensory qualities of dullness or tameness. And this synthesizing of a chaotic world and self in experience is the most basic, the most primordial, instance and meaning of beauty.

If that is the case, how can one say that beauty is being? If beauty is simply experience, something subjective, and if experiencing and being are not identical, how *can* beauty be being? So far, Whitehead's philosophy has sounded like a repetition of the subjective turn of so much of modern philosophy. But it turns out to be something quite different. Rooted in, but not restricted to, human experience, Whitehead's account here aims at a speculative account of the primordial structure of the world itself. What we call the world is fundamentally a flow of occasions of experience through time. And, for Whitehead, experience is not a term for simply an enclosed subjectivity, a mass of feelings, motivations and inner qualities. To experience is to feelingly synthesize data received from the past, the immediate present and various possibilities and ideals. Experience, then, is continually opened out of itself, able to transcend being reduced to the past and its causalities, and opened towards current states of affairs. The 'objective' world exists in Whitehead, but as a flow of sensibility. It is a flow of experiencing units, micro entities that constitute everything that is actual, entities which combine in, and constitute, the complexity of more inclusive units (societies, nexuses).

We see now why Whitehead's aesthetic metaphysics perpetuates and transmutes the great theory. Beauty is symmetry. It comes about as an ordering, a resolution, a synthesis. And we can see how Whitehead has departed from the great theory. Beauty is not just the outcome, the order itself, but a movement that both resolves chaos to order and yet introduces novelty into that very act of resolution. Beauty as both synthesis and intensity of experience is the primordial and universal creativity of world process. It is the creative advance into novelty that is primary beauty. Being – that is, creativity – is beautiful. Whitehead's process metaphysics has thus combined the pre-Hellenic

(Homeric) theogonies with Hellenic Platonism, but his universe flows through time as a synthesizing force that at least partially reduces the chaos of unrelated entities and feelings to both stabilizing experience (memory, perception, feeling and satisfaction) and coherent, societal entities that can endure over time. He has also combined the two motifs that the great theory had difficulty placing into coherent relation: the motifs of objective beauty (proportion, symmetry) and experience (pleasure, delight).

As we would expect, the Whiteheadian aesthetic of coherent creative stability and intensity of feeling is at the same time a way of understanding evil. Evil tags along as the corruption or failure of both sides of beauty. It is thus the element of incoherence that fails to obtain synthesis and interrelation, states of affairs whose actualization adjusts the interests of various competing elements to each other, and an experiential loss of intensity, a dullness that attends mere repetition of the past and failure to obtain new intense satisfactions.

Beauty as Being

In the classical Western theory of beauty and its Whiteheadian transmutation, beauty is never merely a beastly moral corruption, cultural accident or superficial layer of the human psyche, but rather the satisfying syntheses and creativities of the flow of world process. Do the sharp differences between the classical and Whiteheadian metaphysics undermine their testimony to beauty as being? The question is an old one. Does philosophy's historical variety and continuing disbursement into schools discredit philosophy? The twentieth century has seen the rise of philosophies built on an affirmative answer to this question – philosophies which see themselves as philosophy's only genuine and final form. Accordingly, the very fact that there is more than one way of thinking of beauty as being – and this analysis is by no means exhaustive – may prompt some to select one of the ways as superior to, and exclusive of, the others, to adopt one of the new therapeutics of philosophy as final, or to abandon 'philosophy' altogether and, correspondingly, with all discourse about beauty as being. I suggest yet another way.

I contended at the beginning of this chapter that beauty as being is neither the invention nor the sole possession of philosophy. 'Beauty as being' may be a philosophical expression, but beneath that expression lies a conviction that shapes the everyday life of virtually every human society. Few societies or human individuals would seriously maintain that the world of their immediate everyday experience is pervasively, unrelievedly and without exception ugly. If that were the case, 'ugly' would have no meaning. Similar difficulties arise with views that maintain, assert or actually argue that nothing in or about the world is true or real – that all, without exception, is deceit or fiction, including, one must suspect, the argument itself. If there are pervasive elements of beauty in everyday life and the world engagements of human beings, then we can expect human beings to have a certain spontaneous resistance to linguistic, cultural, scientific or philosophical theories which regard everyday human experience as so utterly flawed and linguistically confused that all sciences and philosophies must abandon it in order to do what they do. On the contrary, all sciences and philosophies – with the possible exception of merely formal, analytic, or empty inquiries – presuppose a certain validity of pre-scientific world engagements. If that is the case, it would seem possible to regard both the classical and the neoclassical (Whiteheadian) ways of thinking of beauty as being as not so much the *source* as the *conceptual articulation* and *confirmation* of pre-philosophical everyday experience. And each interpretation expresses a different aspect or dimension of everyday experience and world engagement. The great theory of being articulates the intrinsically satisfying experience of the resplendent proportion of things, that which prompted Emerson to say that 'beauty is its own excuse for being'.[37] The Whiteheadian reinterpretation adds to the great theory the intensity of experience that attends the synthesis of disparate data over the flow of time. Both texts formulate things that all human beings experience in everyday life. Accordingly, because beauty is an intrinsic element in the human experience of life and the world, and thus does not arise simply in philosophical contemplation, we say that 'beauty is being'. The two philosophies express why this is so. One can, of course, delve into the two ways of thinking to discover their conceptual and methodological incompatibilities, but a focus on conceptual incompatibilities – the tendency of any and all philosophical ideologies – carries the high price of wrenching philosophies loose from their attempt to interpret the pre-scientific human engagements with the world. Restored to that task, the differences between philosophies are not absolute.

This chapter qualifies and amends the initial chapter on the suppression of beauty in religious tradition and postmodern culture. In one sense, beauty is passing out of language and, in a vulgarized culture, is reduced to the banality of prettiness. It is suppressed in prevailing ways of interpreting and under-standing the world and in most postmodern institutions. But because the world itself, in its resplendent proportions, its experiential and living flux and its embodied movements, remains beautiful, these suppressions mute, but do not eliminate, beauty.

Notes

1   Ben Jonson, 'The Masque of Beauty', *The Complete Poems* (Harmondsworth: Penguin Books, 1975), p. 297.
2   Alfred North Whitehead, *Process and Reality* (New York: The Macmillan Co., 1929), p. 427.
3   Walter de la Mare, 'The Song of the Secret', *Rhymes and Verses: Collected Poems for Children* (New York: H. Holt, 1947), p. 295.
4   Edna Saint Vincent Millay, 'My Heart Being Hungry', *Collected Lyrics of Edna Saint Vincent Millay* (New York: Harper and Row, 1969), p. 111.
5   A.N. Whitehead, *Process and Reality*, pp. 4–7; *Adventures in Ideas* (Cambridge: Cambridge University Press, 1935), Chapter IX.
6   Wladyslaw Tatarkiewicz, 'The Great Theory of Beauty and its Decline', *Journal of Aesthetics and Art Criticism*, **XXXI** (Winter, 1972), pp. 165–80.
7   According to Tartarkiewicz, Boethius is the mediator of the 'great theory' to the Middle

Ages. Thus Boethius can define beauty as '*commensuratio partium*'. Another important mediator is Pseudo-Dionysius who speaks of beauty's 'proportion' and 'brilliance', two of the three main concepts of the Thomist aesthetic.

8   According to Thomas Aquinas, being is that which, being seen, pleases (*id quod visum placet*). See Jacques Maritain, *Art and Scholasticism*, trans. J.F. Scanlan (New York: Scribner's Sons, 1942), Chapter 5.

9   Ibid., Chapter 3.

10   Samuel Taylor Coleridge, 'The Aeolian Harp', *Selected Poetry and Prose* (New York: Holt, Rinehart and Winston, 1961), p. 15.

11   For a full account of the Orphic theogonies, see Martin L. West, *The Orphic Poems* (Oxford: Clarendon Press, 1983). See also Robert Graves, *The Greek Myths*, Vol. I (Harmondsworth: Penguin Books, 1955), Chapters 1 and 2.

12   Hesiod's *Theogony* is the great systematizing cosmogony of the Homeric period. See Hesiod, *Theognis*, trans. D. Wender (Harmondsworth: Penguin Books, 1973), and, Graves, *The Greek Myths*. Other cosmogonies of ancient Greece and Rome can be found in Apollodorus, *The Library*, Vol. I, trans. E. Fraser (Cambridge, MA: Harvard University Press, 1930), Book I; and Ovid, *The Metamorphoses of Ovid*, trans. M. Innes (Harmondsworth: Penguin Books, 1955), Book I.

13   See Robert Graves, *The White Goddess: A Historical Grammar of Poetic Myth* (New York: Farrar Straus and Giroux, 1975), Chapter IV.

14   In the *Theogony* of Hesiod the children of Ouranos (sky), the Titans, spread destruction and propagate fearful progeny that pervade the world and human experience: Dark Night, Blame, Nemesis, Deceit, Age, Strife, Famine, Murder, Lawlessness, Distress. The victory of Zeus and the Olympians over the Titans, those uncontrollable powers of chaos, did not eliminate these things from the world. The theme of the struggle between chaos and order did not disappear in the early Christian authors. Thus, St Augustine asks, 'Why is it that this part of the universe alternates between deprivation and fulfillment, between discord and harmony?': *Confessions*, Book VIII, Chapter 2.

15   Ovid, *The Metamorphoses of Ovid*, p. 31.

16   Hesiod, *Theognis*, p. 27. Chaos 'was first of all'. Then appeared Earth (the place of the gods), Tartarus, and Eros, 'the most beautiful of all the deathless gods'. And it is Eros that helped chaos give birth to Night, Day, Space, Heaven and so on.

17   Ben Jonson (1572–1637) gives poetic expression to the element of beauty in the Hesiod *Theogony*.

> So Love, emergent out of chaos, brought
> The world to light!
> And gently moving on the waters, wrought
> All form to sight!
> Love's appetite
> Did beauty first excite.

('Euclid's Hymn', *The Complete Poems*, p. 331).

18   In addition to Plato's *Phaedrus*, see his *Symposium*. In this dialogue Plato explicitly cites Hesiod's assertion that Eros is the most beautiful of the gods. He then alters and demythologizes Hesiod, arguing (at least as Socrates) that Eros is a desire or striving that not only surges through the cosmos but also the human soul. As such, it is an intermediary power (a daemon) between the divine and the human, the very fact of desire or urge towards the good. In the soul it is pregnant, tending towards birth, and what it would engender is the beautiful thing. The highest form of Eros, then, is the urge of the soul's knowledge towards the laws of things – towards 'the great sea of beauty', or beauty itself: *The Symposium of Plato*, trans. Suzy Groden (Amherst: University of Massachusetts Press, 1970), pp. 56–57, 91–93.

     For interpretations of Plato on beauty (and the arts), see Bernard Bosanquet, *A History of Aesthetics* (London: Allen and Unwin, 1922), Chapter II; Monroe Beardsley, *Aesthetics from Classical Greece to the Present* (University: University of Alabama Press, 1975),

Chapters 1–3; and Iris Murdoch, *The Fire and the Sun* (Oxford: Clarendon Press, 1977); A.H. Armstrong, 'The Divine Enhancement of Earthly Beauties: The Hellenic and Platonic Tradition', in Herbert Read, *Beauty and the Beast* (Dallas: Spring Publications, 1987). See also Richard Viladesau, *Theological Aesthetics: God in Imagination, Beauty, and Art*, (New York: Oxford University Press, 1999), p. 183.

19   See Plotinus, *Enneads*, trans. A.H. Armstrong (Cambridge, MA: Harvard University Press, 1984), Ennead 1.6 and V.8. See also Bosanquet, *A History of Aesthetics*, Chapter IV.

20   Plotinus, *Enneads*, Ennead 1.6., 1.

21   A few important works on beauty and aesthetics in the Middle Ages are the following. The standard work is Edgar De Bruyne, *Études d'ésthetique médievale* 3 vols. (Bruges: 1946). For an abridged English version, see Edgar De Bruyne, *The Esthetics of the Middle Ages*, trans. E.B. Hennessy (New York: Frederick Ungar, 1969). In addition, see Katherine Gilbert and Helmut Kuhn, *A History of Aesthetics* (2nd edn), (Bloomington, Ind.: Indiana University Press, 1953), Chapter 5; Jacques Maritain, *Art and Scholasticism*; and J.A. Aertsen, 'Beauty in the Middle Ages, a Forgotten Transcendental', *Medieval Philosophical Theology*, I (1991), pp. 68–97. Two of the most detailed studies available, especially focusing on beauty, are Umberto Eco, *The Aesthetics of Thomas Aquinas*, trans. H. Bredin (Cambridge, MA: Harvard University Press, 1988); and his *Art and Beauty in the Middle Ages*, trans. H. Bredin (New Haven, CT: Yale University Press, 1986). (This work was written originally for the four-volume, *Momenti e problemi di storia dell' estetica* (1959).) *Art and Beauty* contains a very extensive and helpful bibliography on medieval aesthetics, pp. 120–29.

22   The most important passages on beauty in Thomas Aquinas are to be found in his commentary on *The Divine Names* of Pseudo-Dionysius. See also *Summa Theologia*, Part I, Q. 5, Art. 1; Q. 39, Art. 8; Part II, Q. 145, Art. 2, and Q. 180, Art. 2 and 3; *Summa contra Gentiles*, Part I, pp. 240, 243. In addition see Albert the Great, 'On Beauty and Good', a work traditionally thought to be by Thomas Aquinas and found in earlier editions of Thomas's works.

23   For St Augustine's notion of concordant harmony and proper order, see *Against the Heathen*, pp. 36–38, *Enchiridion*, Chapter 10–11; 'On Free Will', XI, p. 32; 'Against the Pagans', Part III, p. 35. In his work, 'On Music', Augustine analyses proportion (*analogia*), tracking the relation between the first four numbers. He then argues that not the event of hearing (or remembering), but that which *ratio* grasps, namely the intervals themselves are superior. And because the soul delights in various balancings, in 'equality and equally measured intervals', it is the units of poetic language such as the iamb or the trochee which are beautiful. Furthermore, any specific entity, an iamb or the poem as a whole, is part of a larger harmony or God's total work, and this, too, because of its intervals is beautiful. There is then a hierarchy of beauty, the highest form being the rule of number which most perfectly shows regularity, number, measure. And all of creation shares in this – a kind of divine arithmetic where the numbers are not temporally arranged. See the English translation of *De Musica* by R. Catesby Taliaferro, *St. Augustine on Music* (Annapolis: The St John's Bookstore, 1939), pp. 29–30, 174–78, 190, 197–98.

24   A.H. Armstrong, 'The Divine Enhancement of Earthly Beauties', p. 48.

25   Duns Scotus Erigena, *Periphyseon*, ed. I.P. Sheldon-Williams (Dublin: Dublin Institute for Advanced Studies: 1968), p. 213, also pp. 207, 211.

26   On the beauty of virtue (*areté*) and the 'inner beauty' of the soul, see Plotinus, *Enneads*, Ennead, I. 6., pp. 2–7. See also Eco, *Art and Beauty*, pp. 10–11. Eco quotes Bernard, 'Pulchrum interius speciosus est omni ornatu extrinseco' ('inner beauty is more comely than the power of Kings'): *The Aesthetics of Thomas Aquinas*, Chapter IV.

27   Maritain, *Art and Scholasticism*, Chapters II and IV.

28   This exposition is taken especially from Eco's *The Aesthetics of Thomas Aquinas*, Chapter IV.

29   Maritain, *Art and Scholasticism*, Chapter 5; Eco, *Aesthetics of Thomas Aquinas*, p. 112.

30   Sir Thomas Browne, *Religio Medici* in *Religio Medici, Hydriotaphia, and the Garden of Cyprus*. ed. R.H.A. Robbins (Oxford: Clarendon Press, 1972), p. 17.

31   Robert Bridges, 'Demeter', *Poetical Works of Robert Bridges* (London: Oxford University Press, 1936), p. 55.

32 For instance, see Etienne Gilson, *The Arts and the Beautiful* (New York: Scribner's, 1965), and Mortimer Adler, *Art and Prudence: A Study in Practical Philosophy* (New York: Longman Greens and Co., 1937).

33 For reasons I do not quite fathom, many of the major secondary sources on Whitehead do not include the theme of beauty and aesthetic experience. Most of those which do, focus more on 'aesthetics' as a distinctive experience. The emphasis, then, is the implication of Whitehead's philosophy for the arts, not beauty as an intrinsic feature of his metaphysics of processing being. One of the earliest and most extensive analyses of the Whitehead aesthetic as a theory of the arts is Donald Sherburne's *A Whiteheadian Aesthetic* (New Haven, CT: Yale University Press, 1961). Sherburne's primary aim is to use Whitehead's conceptual scheme to display aesthetic experience as 'aesthetic re-creation', correlated with the arts. Beauty is an intrinsic feature (the mutual adaptation of factors) in all occasions of experience, but one can experience the beautiful without any impulse to re-create, hence the beautiful is not necessarily the aesthetic (Chapter 7). John Cobb's (1957) earlier analysis likewise focuses on aesthetic experience as a distinctive way of relating to objects, and his primary examples come from the arts (painting, music). Since beauty has to do with the subjective form of the apprehensions of patterned relations, as in colours and sounds, it is an aspect of all experience. At the same time, Cobb does not restrict the notion of 'aesthetic object' or 'aesthetic field' simply to art objects. Thus, in Cobb's interpretation, aesthetics as an art-related experience is a distinctive experience but shares in features of a larger aesthetic orientation that comes with experience itself. See John Cobb, 'Toward Clarity in Aesthetics', *Philosophy and Phenomenological Research*, **8** (1957), pp. 169–87.

Other monographs on aesthetic perception and the arts are Bertram Morris, 'The Art Process and the Aesthetic Fact in Whitehead's Philosophy', in Paul A. Schilpp (ed.), *The Philosophy of Alfred North Whitehead* (Evanston: Northwestern University Press, 1941); Eva Schaper, 'Aesthetic Perception', in Ivor Leclerc (ed.), *The Relevance of Whitehead* (New York: Humanities Press, 1961), pp. 263–88; and Jude D. Weisenbeck, *Alfred North Whitehead's Philosophy of Values* (Waukosha, WI: Mount St Pauls College, 1969), Chapter 4; Nathaniel Lawrence, 'The Vision of Beauty in the Temporality of Deity in Whitehead's Philosophy', in George Kline (ed.), *Alfred North Whitehead: Essays in His Philosophy* (Englewood Cliffs, NJ: Prentice-Hall, 1963). All these authors discern in Whitehead a distinction between a broader sense of aesthetic perception (aesthetic intuition, aesthetic fact) which attends concrescence itself and the more distinctive art-related aesthetic experience. The major work that constructs a *theological* aesthetic on the basis of Whitehead's conceptual scheme is William Dean's *Coming To: A Theology of Beauty* (Philadelphia: Westminster Press, 1972).

34 Whitehead's philosophy of beauty and aesthetic experience can be found in a variety of passages in *Process and Reality* (1929). More specifically, see *Adventures of Ideas* (London: Cambridge University Press, 1933), Chapter XVII; *Modes of Thought* (New York: Macmillan Co., 1938), Chapter 3; and *Science and the Modern World* (New York: Macmillan Co., 1967), Chapter XIII.

35 Whitehead, *Modes of Thought*, Chapter 1.

36 Charles Hartshorne follows Whitehead in the attempt to overcome the rift between subjective and objective locations of beauty. See 'The Aesthetic Matrix of Value', in *Creative Synthesis and Philosophic Method* (LaSalle, IL: Open Court, 1970).

37 Ralph Waldo Emerson, 'The Rhodora', *Poems* (London and Toronto: J.M. Dent, 1914), p. 31.

Chapter 3

Beauty as Sensibility

For what is beauty, if it does not fire the loving answer of an eager soul. (Robert Bridges)[1]

Though it be certain that beauty and deformity, more than sweet and bitter, are not qualities in objects but belong entirely to the sentiment internal and external, it must be allowed that there are certain qualities in objects which are fitted by nature to produce those particular feelings. (David Hume)[2]

Beauty is a notion of the mind, accompanied by pleasure but a notion founded on something real, existing outside us. (Denis Diderot)[3]

In the Western texts we find a tale of beauty, not simply a miscellany of interpretations. At the beginning of that tale, beauty is said to come with being, and 'to be' (as cosmos, entity, order) is 'to be beautiful'. The tale ends with texts that discover beauty in human self-transcendence and human world engagement. Both moments, beauty as being and beauty as human self-transcendence, are important for a theological aesthetic: the former as a way of articulating an intrinsic property of creation (and nature), the latter as a way of understanding the human being as the corruption and redemption of the divine image. These two moments offer up complementary insights rather than exclusive theories of beauty, and in Chapter 5 I shall explore texts that assign to beauty an important role in human self-transcendence and world engagement. However, something happened in the Western interpretation of beauty between these two moments. In eighteenth-century England a group of authors whose writings appeared in or around the 1750s challenged the classical and medieval 'great theory' of beauty[4] and laid the groundwork for those who located beauty in and as human self-transcendence. Later interpretations (romanticism, transcendental philosophy and phenomenology) are made possible by this eighteenth-century discovery of beauty as a sensibility.

The eighteenth-century texts on beauty do not begin in a historical vacuum: they share the Renaissance suspicion of metaphysics and follow its humanistic turn. Even if an impenetrable veil had fallen between human beings and the ultimate mystery of things, the strange mystery of human beings themselves remained – a mystery that fascinated Descartes and engendered the birth of modern philosophy. Twentieth-century critics of Descartes and Cartesianism – and that includes virtually all intellectual movements – are so repulsed by Descartes' 'dualism' that they miss his primary accomplishment, the articulation of the non-reducibility of the human (the personal and the subjective) to sheer quantity. Descartes articulated what all objectifying claims presuppose: human experience and the activities of consciousness. Thus began centuries of philosophical inquiry that would expose, map or thematize the human being itself: its 'inner senses' (Locke); transcendental accomplishments (Kant); passionate subjectivity (Kierkegaard); and world-engaging structure (Heidegger). The eighteenth-century turn to psychology or fundamental anthropology is the larger event that created the new problematic of beauty[5] which gave rise to both a new set of questions about beauty and the relocation of beauty in and as a human sensibility – for instance, what is beauty's psychological origin and possibility, what is beauty's place among the various human emotions and dispositions, and how can there be standards for beauty's claims?

Precursors of the Eighteenth-century Turn

As already stated, mid-eighteenth-century England and Europe produced a group of rather startling texts that articulated a new problematic of beauty,[6] although hints of this new problematic were already present in the philosophy of Descartes and some of his successors. For purposes of illustration only, I shall select four precursors of the eighteenth-century turn, two from the sixteenth century (René Descartes and Michel de Montaigne) and two from the seventeenth century (Francis Bacon and Thomas Hobbes). Each figure qualifies or supplements the great theory of beauty as an objective property (proportion, harmony) of things. The work of these precursors includes the relocation of beauty into human passions (Descartes, Hobbes), an agnosticism about the character of beauty (Montaigne), the cultural relativity of judgements about bodily beauty (Montaigne), and the denial that beauty is merely ordered pattern (Bacon).

Descartes' philosophy of human emotions and their 'inner sense', and his discovery of beauty's connection with desire, represented a fundamental shift that anticipated what was to come.[7] Montaigne says quite explicitly that we do not 'know what beauty is in nature'.[8] People all agree that fire is hot: they do not agree that a specific kind of body or face is beautiful. Beauty is thus a culturally varied value. Montaigne, however, does not press this theme of beauty's relativity to a consistent conclusion. He presupposes a kind of universal hierarchy or scale of beauty when he argues that the *human* body is not the most beautiful body among animals. Francis Bacon departs from the great theory of beauty when he explicitly denies that beauty is mere proportion: a 'strangeness of proportion', as for instance a 'decent and gracious motion' is more beautiful than a strict pattern. Thus 'felicity', not mere rule, is the more important criterion by which to judge the work of painters and musicians. And, while Bacon does not actually relocate beauty into human dispositions, he takes a step in that direction by arguing for a 'natural' correlation between physical beauty and virtue, between physically beautiful people and beautiful spirit. Here beauty is not yet itself spirit, something in or about the subject, but neither is it merely an external property.[9]

Thomas Hobbes not only anticipates the Lockean and Humean project of discovering the way in which human dispositions are organized but, like Descartes, he actually locates beauty by analysing the passions. He begins by distinguishing among the emotions appetite and aversion, the objects of which are good and evil. He then identifies three kinds of good, the *utile* or profitable good – good as the means of something – *jucundum* or some desired end, and *pulchrum* or the beautiful as a mien or countenance or 'apparent sign' for a promised good. Accordingly, a face is beautiful that manifests or signals a good to come.[10] The importance of this very brief and obscure passage is the location of beauty (*pulchrum*) as the object of a distinctive human appetite and the attempt to distinguish beauty from the useful and from immediate pleasure. Hobbes thus anticipates Hume's much more complicated analysis of beauty's operation in human dispositions and his denial that beauty is simply a sensation of pleasure.

The New Problematic of Beauty in the Eighteenth Century

Three motifs constitute what I am calling the new problematic of beauty: the relocation of beauty from an external property to a human sensibility (which created the problematic), the problem of taste, and the recovery of the ancient concept of the sublime. All three themes are articulated by two early eighteenth-century English thinkers: John Dennis and Joseph Addison. In Dennis, the three themes arise in connection with his comprehensive critical analysis of poetry.[11] Anticipating Hume, Dennis distinguishes passions which respond to immediate objects (Hume would call this sensation) and passions evoked by ideas (Hume will call this reflective impressions). In his view, beauty means the regularity of things and thus the arts (poetry) embody this regularity by keeping to certain rules. Implied here, but not explicitly stated, is the notion that the beauty (regularity) of poetry evokes the passions. But beauty itself is not yet relocated in the passions. In addition, Dennis is said to be the first to attempt a definition of taste and he is also the first among the English to significantly recover the ancient motif of the sublime, an important theme in his *Grounds of Criticism in Poetry* (1704).

All three themes also appear in Joseph Addison's *Spectator* essays.[12] Addison may have been the first modern to propose what became a standard way of organizing human psychological faculties into a triad of the understanding, the senses and the imagination.[13] He goes further than Dennis in transplanting beauty from an external property to an inward disposition, placing the imagination, or fancy, between the senses and the understanding, and then identifying three pleasures of the imagination, one of which is beauty.[16] The point seems to be that beauty is manifested in connection with a distinctive imaginative pleasure, and because the imagination itself is continually engaged with the specific furnishings of the world, this pleasure requires a visual object. In addition, Addison offered his own analysis both of taste (as 'fine taste') and the sublime which he discusses using the term 'greatness'.

The Psychological Relocation of Beauty

The transplantation of beauty from objective pattern to a category of experience began as early as Descartes and continued in relatively undeveloped form in Hobbes, Dennis and Addison. More detailed treatments of beauty as a human sensibility would come only with more elaborate and detailed psychologies of the human faculties. In England John Locke paved the way for a new philosophical psychology, thus creating a method and framework for Francis Hutcheson and David Hume.[15]

Hutcheson, whose work on beauty falls chronologically between Addison and Hume, expresses the motif of relocation in the very title of his book, *An Inquiry into the Original of Our Ideas of Beauty and Virtue* (1725). This title reflects the eighteenth-century fascination with genealogical psychology, the psychological origination of things in the 'inner senses'.[16] Thus arise 'genealogies' (Nietzsche) of beauty that track beauty's origin and site in the human psyche. Hutcheson follows Dennis in distinguishing the 'powers of perception' from mere 'sensations' which arise as immediate bodily responses (such as seeing and hearing) to external actions. In *perception* intellectual activities operate to synthesize and compare ideas. Beauty arises not as a sensation but as 'an idea rais'd in us' – thus, the appeal of a sunset, or a fine face. A 'sense of beauty' is one of the powers of perception, the power of receiving that idea. Note that both sides of the distinction, beauty itself (an idea) and the sense of beauty (a psychological power) are *immanent* psychological phenomena. Hutcheson thus builds on, but elaborates, Dennis and Addison. Beauty is not a passive sensation of something external – for instance, the hearing of a sound – but is a certain kind of perceptiveness which is strong in some and weak in others, and this sense of beauty is possible only if there is some meant content (idea). Beauty, then, is 'the perception of some mind'.[17]

David Hume, writing 15 or so years after Hutcheson, picks up all these themes. What is little more than a brief suggestion in Hobbes – namely, that beauty arises as a 'good' correlated with a human appetite – becomes in Hume an extended psychological analysis of beauty's origin and location. Once beauty was reassigned to the passions and dispositions of a subject, it became a standard theme of philosophical psychology which is especially borne out in David Hume's *Treatise on Human Nature* (1739–40).[18] Although Hume was not a reductionistic subjectivist, he did attempt to sort out the activities, dispositions and feelings of the human psyche. Concerned not to reduce the human being to a knowing machine, Hume tried to understand the whole passionate life of the human being – that is, the sensibilities oriented to pleasure and pain that knowing presupposes. Beauty, then, is not an external property but a human disposition, a special kind of sensibility. What kind? Hume is clear that it is not a *cognitive* sensibility, an element of the act of knowing; echoing Descartes and Hobbes, he says that beauty arises in the human passions. But passions are not mere sensations (original impressions). One type of passion is a *reflective* impression, and reflective impressions comprise both emotions and ideas. The emotions that accompany reflective impressions can be calm or violent. Only at this point is Hume ready to locate beauty as a human disposition. The sense of beauty arises when human beings at some reflective (idea-laden) level emotionally experience something that is 'calmly' delightful or pleasurable.

Like Hutcheson, Hume did not abandon the great theory and motif of proportion. As a reflective impression, beauty's delight is evoked by objects that have 'an order or construction of parts'.[19] But unlike Hutcheson, who emptied beauty of all elements of utility, Hume argued that it is utility that makes the references of beauty more than just pattern or structure. Thus, we take delight not just in the manifest and geometrical structure of a palace or an animal but in the functions fulfilled by the palace's designs and the functional agility of the animal. Accordingly, the body's beauty is not mere pattern but a combination of strength or power and various utilities or bodily capabilities in which human beings take pride.[20]

The Problem of Taste

Insofar as beauty is an objective property of things, it can evoke a variety of proposals about just what that property is: harmony, proportion, fitness, unity in difference. With beauty's relativization into cultural differences (Montaigne), arises a new problem which is greatly intensified by beauty's transportation into the realm of the passions and dispositions. For, as a psychological phenomenon, an experience, discernment or imaginative reflection, beauty will vary not simply among different cultures but in the psychologies of individuals. This is why the shift to the subjective carried with it the motif and problem of taste. Accordingly, we find Dennis, Addison, Hutcheson and Hume, as well as their mid-century successors, all addressing the question of taste.[21]

After three centuries of cultural and personal relativization, taste has now become a term for the arbitrary aesthetic preferences of individuals: 'Judgments of taste are non-disputable' as the old adage goes. But for the early eighteenth-century authors the concept of taste was more a way of preventing the complete subjectification of beauty than an expression of that subjectification itself.[22] Beauty may be threatened by apparent cultural differences and its location in the passions; taste, or at least 'refined taste', halted the slide into utter relativity.[23] The problem of taste, then, was the problem of the 'standards of taste' (Hume), of how a disciplined, refined taste may come about. The search was for 'rules' of taste either immanent in the human being itself or manifest in certain objective properties to which discernment was attuned.[24]

Taste as a serious issue entered English criticism with John Dennis and Joseph Addison. Dennis is the first to offer a definition: taste is 'the organ of perception of literary things'.[25] For Addison, 'fine taste' implies an objectivity – that is, rules that measure such taste. In his view, taste is 'that faculty of the soul which discerns the Beauty of an Author with pleasure and the imperfection with Dislike'.[26] These initial proposals set the stage for Hume and Gerard.[27] For both these authors, 'refined taste' is what prevents individuals' variable sensations, appetites and sentiments from being absolute. They agree that taste itself is a capacity or power of the human self to perceive beauty. Thus, it is a 'delicacy of the imagination', a 'sensibility to beauty and deformity' (Hume), a term for what can improve the powers of the imagination (Gerard).

Accordingly, as a power, or a discernment, taste has an element of judgement and thus standards. This concern for standards leads these authors to reconnect themselves with the ancient tradition of beauty as proportion and as a property in things – a tradition that was not totally abandoned in the eighteenth-century psychological relocation of beauty. To justify and ground their notions of discernments, judgements and standards, Hume and Gerard needed something which was not a human disposition to which the discernments were oriented and by which they could be said to be 'refined'. That something was the concept of *standards* of taste by way of which the objective references and properties of beauty are restored. In Hume's view, even though there were widespread differences about what was beautiful and what was deformed, these 'sentiments' were rooted in 'certain qualities of objects which are fitted by nature to produce these particular feelings'. Hume does not offer a detailed account of these properties. Instead, citing instances of writing, he argues that there are self-evident principles of composition and general rules that apply thereto.

Hogarth's *Analysis of Beauty* (1753) is not a work on taste, but it does address the problem of objective standards. He discerns a certain kind of empathetic act (imagination) in which one grasps the object as if one were internal to it. But what is grasped as (visually) beautiful is a collection of features: the fitness of parts to the whole, regularity and symmetry, intricacy, lines and proportion. Hogarth moves beyond the great theory of beauty not by a return to the subjective but by a detailed elaboration of multiple properties which together constitute beauty.[28]

In sum, the motif of taste served as a correction of the subjectivist tendencies to identify beauty with a psychological 'inner' phenomenon. Beauty, then, is not simply a referentless passion, an inner disposition. These dispositions are at the same time perceptions which can be disciplined (refined) to correspond to certain non-subjective properties in nature or in the arts, which properties account for the pleasure felt in beauty as a sentiment.

The Sublime

If the motif of taste served to anchor the subjectivism that was inherent in locating beauty in the passions, another motif arose to qualify the dominance of standards and rules. The eighteenth-century English authors were correlationists, discovering a correspondence between beauty as a sensibility and the objective properties that evoked it. But is beauty strictly and exhaustively the pleasurable discernment of order, proportion, and even fitness? Something seems to be omitted from such an analysis. The human experience of at least certain kinds of beautiful things – such as a mountain massif or a starry sky – has an element in it that is not sheer pleasure. From the beginning of the eighteenth century through Kant and his successors, a set of authors appropriated Longinus's notion, the sublime, to express this transpleasurable element.[29]

Longinus, a third-century Greek philosopher and rhetorician in the Platonic tradition, had written a work on 'the height' (sublime) whose theme was the elevation, transportation, and excitement stimulated by certain poetic devices.[30] In this work the sublime posed an issue of rhetorical strategy and style, something the poet can do to overcome the human being's resistance to self-transcending emotional involvement. But the eighteenth-century English authors, working within the conceptual frame of Lockean psychological methods, were preoccupied with human sentiments and dispositions. For them, the sublime named not a rhetorical problem but a distinctive experience, or something that evoked that experience.[31] The first English author to make the sublime a central category altered the meaning of the sublime by way of an explicit criticism of Longinus.[32] For John Dennis, the sublime describes not so much rhetoric and language but a distinctive way in which human beings are emotionally engaged with what impinges on them. Human beings are passionately engaged at more than one level. Common (vulgar) passions are more or less spontaneous reactions to stimuli, such as anger. 'Enthusiastic passions' have a core of ideas (meanings, contents) that prompt joy, horror or terror. The sublime is a passion of the latter type, and it is aroused by something sufficiently awesome or threatening to evoke terror. For Dennis, the primary object of the sublime is God, the ultimate mystery and threat to finite, evil-doing human beings.

Most influential of all the English texts is Edmund Burke's 1756 work on the sublime and the beautiful.[33] The work is not so much a break with the previous 50 years of interpretations, such as those of Dennis, as a more focused and detailed analysis of the sublime as a distinctive experience. In Burke's view, the sublime names not a specific passion but something referential and objective, hence his phrase 'the passion caused by the sublime'. Burke identifies a range of entities that evoke to a lesser or greater degree the terrors of the sublime: wild animals, the majesty of monarchs, the vastness of the ocean. But what carries his analysis beyond the others is his correlation between certain qualities of these entities and the emotions they arouse. Thus, what evokes terror, astonishment, awe, horror and the like is not just the entity, ocean or tiger, but a sensed infinity, vastness, privation, darkness and magnificence. These terms describe neither the emotions themselves nor the specific entities but something that renders the entities awesome. Similarly, certain contemporary philosophers would speak of nothingness as coming with being and the human participation in being. The sublime then names neither something subjective nor objective but rather a way in which certain human emotions are seized by a dimension of things that human beings cannot control, predict, be secure with or even conceptualize.

For Burke and others, the sublime names a dimension of things correlated to a distinctive experience that is differentiated from beauty. This opposition between beauty and the sublime presupposes that beauty is a *pleasurable* sensibility or discernment and its reference is something orderly or fitting. In Burke's words, beauty is 'that quality or those qualities in bodies by which they love, or some passion similar to it'.[34] If beauty has to do with an attractiveness that evokes pleasure, such an opposition is inevitable. On the other hand, the sublime could relate to beauty not as an alternative experience but as a dimension of beauty itself – that which reveals something about the experience of the beautiful that is not mere pleasure. A mountain massif may be sublime but it is not simply unbeautiful. Its sublimity adds a dimension of mystery, depth and even pathos to the experience of the beautiful. Given the finite character of all beautiful things, it is difficult to imagine any entity in which pathos and mystery are utterly absent. The sublime thus reveals beauty as a sensibility to be a mix of pleasure and pathos.

Legacies and Ambiguities

It is difficult to overstate the importance of the early and middle eighteenth century in the story and legacy of beauty. The eighteenth century is important because it set in motion two almost opposite historical outcomes. One strand of events and texts was a new vision of beauty in the Western tradition that moved beyond the classical Hellenic and medieval view. This vision itself had multiple historical aspects. It created a new criticism and a new autonomy of *beaux arts*. Because of the centrality of the passions and the element of mystery (the sublime), it engendered the 'romantic' side of neoclassicism itself and gave the Romantic movement many of its features. Because its texts included not just criticism (of poetry and the arts) but philosophy, its predecessors were also Descartes, Hobbes and Locke and its successors Kant, the German idealists, Kierkegaard, and Schopenhauer. Placed in this strand of history, the texts on beauty and the sublime serve as a moment in philosophy's ever renewed grappling with the question of human self-transcendence. The English texts do not use the term, self-transcendence, but their depiction of human passionate life as constituted, at least in part, by beauty is at the same time an account of the irreducibility of the human being to external causalities. Passionately engaged with the beautiful, the human being is not simply a thinking machine, a biological accident or an economic statistic. And it was the eighteenth century's location of beauty as part of the passionate life of human beings that expressed this transcendence.

We must also acknowledge that the eighteenth century's location of beauty among human sensibilities had another long-term outcome: it sowed the seeds of beauty's eventual demise in Western aesthetics. A persisting ambiguity dogged these texts, the two sides of which are explicitly set out by David Hume. 'Beauty and deformity', he says, 'are not qualities of objects but belong entirely to the sentiment internal and external.' Shifting to the other side, he also can speak of 'obvious beauties that strike the senses'.[35] If beauty belongs entirely to the sentiment, what is it that 'strike the senses'? Surely not the sentiment? These statements are typical of the literature, which both locates beauty in and as a human passion (or discernment) and speaks of objective beauties. I used the term, correlation, to describe this view, but the term only highlights the ambiguity. What in fact *is* beauty and where does it reside? A subject–object psychology still reigns in these texts and will not be explicitly challenged until Schopenhauer who argues against both objective and subjective locations of beauty.

Judged by historical outcome, the ambiguity was not a trivial one. Only two things could have resolved it, given the psychology and metaphysical framework of the period. It could be resolved by falling back to the classical view – beauty as (structure, proportion) being. Or it could be resolved by placing beauty simply in the subject and accepting the relativizing consequences. This, in fact, is the tendency of the period, and what prevented the utter relativization of beauty were the proposed standards of taste. But taste and its standards were themselves vulnerable to the changes and criticisms of future generations. Taste itself became relativized and, with that, beauty was drawn into the morass of the human psyche and the endless varieties of human culture. The artist, then, could do without it and so could the critic, the aesthetician and the philosopher. Reduced to an immanent emotion and a psychological variable, beauty lost its power to express human self-transcendence. It would be assigned to one side of various dualisms: beauty opposed to the ethical, beauty opposed to faith, beauty opposed even to the aesthetic. Chapter 1 offered a brief version of the end of the story – the loss of the beauty in the postmodern period. In the following chapters I shall pick up the other side, the legacy and promise of the eighteenth century – the power of beauty to evoke and constitute human self-transcendence.

Notes

1 Robert Bridges, 'Eros and Psyche', *The Poetical Works of Robert Bridges* (London: Oxford University Press, 1936), p. 98.

2 David Hume, 'Of the Standard of Taste', in J.W. Lenz (ed.), *Of the Standard of Taste and Other Essays* (Indianapolis: Bobbs-Merrill, 1965), p. 11.

3 Denis Diderot, cited in Monroe Beardsley, 'Beauty', in Philip Wiener (ed.), *Dictionary of the History of Ideas*, Vol. 1, (New York: Scribner's, 1968), p. 199.

4 In addition to the standard histories of aesthetics (Bosanquet, Gilbert and Kuhn, Beardsley), the following works are especially helpful for the eighteenth century. An excellent compact history of the major European texts is the essay, '(Die) Schöne', in Joachim Ritter and Karlfried Gründer (eds), *Historisches Wörterbuch der Philosophie*, Vol. 8, (Basel: Schwabe, 1992). See also Jerome Stolnitz, 'Beauty: Some Stages in the History of an Idea', *Journal of the History of Ideas*, **XXX** (January–March, 1962). See also the following monographs: Walter Hipple jr, *The Beautiful, the Sublime, and the Picturesque in 18th Century British Aesthetic Theory* (Carbondale, IL: Southern Illinois Press, 1957); and Paul Oskar Kristeller, *Renaissance Thought II* (Princeton, NJ: Princeton University Press, 1980), Chapter IX.

5 The following statement from Walter Hipple jr's study of eighteenth-century aesthetics serves as a succinct articulation of the new problematic of beauty.

> The aestheticians of this period all found their subject to be psychological: the central problem for them was not some aspect of the cosmos or of the particular substances, nor was it found among the characteristics of human activity, or of the modes of symbolic representation; one and all, they found their problem to be the specification and discrimination of certain kinds of feelings, the determination of the mental powers and susceptibilities which yielded those feelings, and of the impressions and ideas which excited them. (p. 305)

6   The major texts in and around the 1750s include M. de L'Isle André, *Essai sur le beauté* (1741); C. Batteux, *Les Beaux Arts* (1746); Alexander Gottlieb Baumgarten's *Aesthetica* (1750); William Hogarth, *The Analysis of Beauty* (1753); David Hume, 'The Standard of Taste' (1757); Edmund Burke, *A Philosophical Inquiry into our Ideas of the Origin of the Sublime and the Beautiful* (1756); and Alexander Gerard, *Essay on Taste* (1759). Furthermore, Jonathan Edwards began work on *The Nature of True Virtue*, a landmark in the theological aesthetics of beauty, while at Stockbridge in 1754.

7   Descartes remained more or less within the 'great theory' of beauty. Thus, he could speak of 'the wondrous beauty of the Universe': *Passions of the Soul* (1649), trans. Stephen Voss (Indianapolis: Hackett Publishing Co., 1989), p. 13. At the same time, his analysis of the human emotions anticipates the psychological turn of the eighteenth century. Using a kind of phenomenological method – that is, a method that would uncover necessary relations between intentional activities of consciousness and their objects – Descartes argued that certain emotions (passions) of love and hatred are correlated with certain types of objects such as goods and evils. But there are distinctive types of object of love. *Goods* are relations to emotions of desire, an 'internal sense'. The *beautiful*, especially as presented by sight, is related to the emotion of *delight* (agreement) mediated by external senses. Because this analysis identifies a particular kind of human emotion differentiated from other kinds – an emotion that arises with the experience of the beautiful – it represents a momentous step towards opening up modern aesthetics. See *Passions of the Soul*, pp. 65–69.

8   'Apology for Raimond de Sebonde', in W.C. Hazlitt (ed.), *The Essays of Michel de Montaigne*, Vol. I (New York: A.L. Burt, nd), p. 472.

9   Sir Francis Bacon, 'Of Beauty', *Essays and Counsels Civill and Morall*, ed. M. Kiernan (Oxford: Oxford University Press, 1985).

10 Thomas Hobbes, *Leviathan* (1651), ed. E. Curley (Indianapolis: Hackett Publishing Co., 1994), Chapter VI, #8.

11 John Dennis, *A Large Account of the Taste in Poetry and the Degeneration of It* (1702) and, *The Grounds of Criticism in Poetry* (1704) in John Dennis, *The Critical Works of John Dennis*, ed. E.N. Hooker (Baltimore: Johns Hopkins Press, 1937), Vol. 1.

12 For an account of Addison on beauty, see Stolnitz, 'Beauty'.

13 The triad of faculties appears in Hume's analysis as the understanding, the passions and morals. It reappears in Immanual Kant's three critiques: the cognitive, the moral (practical) and the aesthetic. Friedrich Schleiermacher continues the line, proposing immediate self-consciousness (*Gefühl*), knowing, and action (*Tun*).

14 Joseph Addison, 'The Pleasures of the Imagination', *Spectator*, (21–23 June, 1712).

15 The focus of this review is on the English texts. In Germany, writing approximately in the period of David Hume, Alexander Gottlieb Baumgarten coined the term, aesthetic, as an inquiry or discipline (*Wissenschaft*) of sense experience. Hume and Locke both undertook extensive analyses of sense experience, although not under the rubric of a new science. Baumgarten had lectured on the subject in the 1740s and published his *Aesthetica* in 1750. Because this new science of sense experience was also a 'metaphysic of the beautiful', Baumgarten is given credit for the turn of European thinking which freed the '*beaux arts*' from their older attachment to techniques and crafts. The independent programme of criticism of the arts (especially of poetry) had already had its inception in Dennis and Addison.

16 Hutcheson proceeds to analyse beauty's place among human disciplines only after he has offered precise criticisms of the traditional, objective approaches to beauty. For a summary of his criticisms, see Stolnitz, 'Beauty', s. III.

17 *An Inquiry into the Original of Our Ideals of Beauty and Virtue*, pp. 14–15.

18 For Hume's analysis of beauty, see *Treatise on Human Nature*, Book II, Section VIII, 'Of Beauty and Deformity'.

19 Ibid., p. 299.

20 It is difficult to know how much influence Hume's interpretation of beauty had on the many English works on beauty that appeared in the 1750s. It does seem evident that many of Hume's themes were picked up by Immanuel Kant: the tripartite analysis of human

faculties (cognitive, moral, passionate); the motif of judgement (the reflective dimension of the aesthetic); taste; and judgement as an element of beauty.

21   Secondary works on the history of the concept of taste abound. See Giorgio Tonelli, 'Taste in the History of Aesthetics from the Renaissance to 1770', in Weiner, *Dictionary of the History of Ideas*, Vol. IV; Hannelore Klein, *There is No Disputation about Taste: Untersuchungen um Englischen Geschmäcksbegriff in Achtzehnten Jahrhunderdt* (Münster: Verlag Aschendorf, 1967); Andrew Canon Smith, *Theories of the Nature and Standard of Taste in England 1706–1770* (Chicago: University of Chicago Press, 1937). Stolnitz, 'Beauty', s. II.

22   The problem of taste was widespread in European letters and was thus not simply a concern of the English authors. According to Tonelli, taste was applied to the problem of beauty in late seventeenth-century France by François La Rochefoucauld. Voltaire, Montesquieu and d'Alembert all wrote articles on taste in the *Encyclopédie*.

23   'Yet each of our writers owed allegiance to the standard, or to a standard, and many – Burke, Gerard, Hume, Lord Kames, Reynolds, Stewart – devised arguments to demonstrate a rightness of taste': Hipple, *The Beautiful, the Sublime, and the Picturesque*, p. 310.

24   D'Alembert succinctly articulated this connection between immanent location and the rules of taste.

> The truth is that the source of our pleasure and of our disgust lies solely and entirely within ourselves; so that, if we reflect with attention upon our mental frame, we shall find there general and invariable rules of *taste* which will serve as the criterion of beauty and deformity. (Quoted in Walter Hipple's 'Introduction' to Alexander Gerard, *An Essay on Taste (1759)*, ed. Walter J. Hipple (Gainsville, Fl.: Scholars' Facsimiles and Reprints, 1963), p. xxii.

25   Klein, *There is No Disputation about Taste*, p. 19.

26   See Joseph Addison, *Spectator* (19 June 1712). According to one commentator, Addison picked up the term 'taste' from Gratin's *Arte de ingénio* (1642).

27   For Hume on taste, see 'Delicacy of Taste', in *Essays and Treatises on Various Subjects*, Vol. I (Edinburgh, 1817) and 'Of the Standard of Taste', in *Of the Standard of Taste and Other Essays*, ed. J.W. Lenz (Indianapolis: Bobbs-Merrill, 1965). For Gerard, see Alexander Gerard, *An Essay on Taste* (1759).

28   Alexander Gerard, possibly drawing on Hogarth, lists the following features of beautiful objects: variety, which gives a sense of novelty; proportion or the aptitude of a structure to its end (cf. Hume's 'utility'); colours; and evidences of design: *Essay on Taste*, Part I, S. III.

29   This literature includes both English and French texts. The theme of the sublime appears in Addison as 'one of the three faculties and types of pleasure ("the great")', thus in this case as something to be distinguished from beauty: *Spectator* (23 June 1712). See also John Dennis, *The Grounds of Criticism in Poetry* (1704); Silvain's *Traité du sublime* (1732); Edmund Burke, *A Philosophical Inquiry*. Kant's great work, *The Critique of Judgment*, which synthesized motifs of taste, judgment, beauty and the sublime, apppeared in 1790.

30   Longinus was first translated into English by Hull in 1652 but little attention was paid to the work. It was the Boileau translation and interpretation of 1674 that stimulated a number of additional translations of *On the Sublime* and began the long period of Longinus's influence on English criticism. See Longinus, *On the Sublime, English and Greek*, ed. W. Rhys Roberts (New York: Garland, 1987). For a brief exposition, see Samuel Monk, *The Sublime: A Study of Critical Theories in XVIII England* (New York: MLAA, 1935), Chapter 1.

31   Samuel Monk's *The Sublime* may be the fullest survey of the motif in English. In addition, see Paul Crowther, 'The Sublime', in *Routledge Encyclopedia of Philosophy* (London/ New York: Routledge, 1998); 'Erhabene', in Ritter and Gründer, *Historiches Wörterbuch*; and Andrew Ashfield and Peter deBolla, *The Sublime: A Reader in 18th Century Aesthetic Theory* (Cambridge: Cambridge University Press, 1996); Hipple, *The Beautiful, the*

Sublime, and the Picturesque; and H.J. Hoffman, *Die Lehre von Erhabenen bei Kant und seinen Vorgängern* (Halle, 1913).

32   John Dennis contended that by reducing the sublime to rhetoric, a matter of language, Longinus contradicted its very nature – namely the terror at work in a human passion. Dennis, *The Grounds of Criticism*, pp. 78–79.

33   Edmund Burke, *A Philosophical Inquiry*, Part II.

34   Ibid., p. 91. Burke does acknowledge that beauty and the sublime can coexist in certain works of art.

35   Hume, 'On the Standard of Taste', p. 11.

Chapter 4

Beauty as Benevolence

Is she kind as she is fair?
For beauty lives with kindness. (William Shakespeare)[1]

Inward beauty is more comely than exterior ornament, more even than the power of Kings. (Saint Bernard)[2]

Benevolence to being in general, or to being simply considered, is entirely a distinct thing from uniformity in the midst of variety and is a superior kind of beauty. (Jonathan Edwards)[3]

As discussed in Chapter 3, the early and middle eighteenth century in England and Europe marked a decisive turn in the history of the interpretation of beauty. The three themes of sensibility, taste and the sublime shaped a new anthropological (psychological) way of understanding how beauty draws the human being out of the circle of self-preoccupation into self-transcendence. At the same time, beauty's vacillating location between a sensibility and an objective property created grounds for its eventual relativization and demise. In the same period a distinctive event took place in the Western tale of beauty. This event was not a movement, trend or controversy, but the aesthetic theology of the New England clergyman, Jonathan Edwards.

Jonathan Edwards (1703–1758) almost never appears in the standard histories of beauty and aesthetics. His role in the Great Awakening and his frequently anthologized sermon depicting sinners in the hands of an angry God suggest to modern religious thinkers that Edwards is someone best ignored. I intend no hyperbole when I say that, in Edwards' interpretation of philosophical and religious themes (God, redemption, evil, human psychology and cosmology), beauty is more central and more pervasive than in any other text in the history of Christian theology. Edwards does not just theologize *about* beauty: beauty (loveliness, sweetness) is the fundamental motif through which he understands the world, God, virtue and 'divine things'. A double irony attends the suppression of Edwards in the history of aesthetics. It is ironical to reduce Edwards' thought to the motif of the avenging God when, for Edwards, beauty is God's primary attribute. And it is ironical to exclude Edwards from the history of aesthetics in face of the fact that, of all the eighteenth-century authors, Edwards marks by far the most original and radical departure from the great theory of beauty.[4]

When we compare Edwards to the early eighteenth-century English texts on beauty, he seems at first sight to simply reproduce both the subjective turn (beauty as a passion and a sensibility) and the correlational view (the correspondence between external proportion or fittingness with a sensibility).

On closer examination, we find that Edwards radicalizes the eighteenth-century turn. The reason why Edwards appears to simply perpetuate Dennis, Hutcheson and others is that he distinguishes primary beauty as a disposition of the heart from secondary beauty which is the proportion and harmony of things: thus the subjective turn and correlation. But something quite different is in fact at work in the Edwards' texts. The eighteenth-century English authors differentiate beauty from mere sensation by locating it in the faculties of the imagination and in (idea-laden) discernment. Sensibility to beauty is the felt discernment of a certain idea as it appears in a melodic line, an ordered object or a line of poetry. Both the legacy of the great theory of beauty and the placement of the theory of beauty in the arts (Dennis, for instance) are at work in these texts. Edwards, on the other hand, will not allow nature, the arts or the classical legacy to be the primary contexts for posing the question of beauty. He *does* agree that the place to look for beauty is what we would now call the order of the personal – the dispositions and passions (affections) of human beings and, at this point, he follows his eighteenth-century English predecessors' relocation of beauty into human experience.[5] To use Edwards' language, beauty's region is 'intelligent beings', the 'mind' and, most specifically, the affections and the heart. In what way, then, does Edwards' view depart from the other eighteenth-century authors?

Primary and Secondary Beauty

In line with his eighteenth-century contemporaries, Edwards' relocation of beauty into the realm of the personal (and moral agency) did not amount to a repudiation of the Hellenic and medieval notion of beauty as conformity and harmony. The world at large, even as comprised of inanimate entities, displays a certain beauty. For what is the world after all but a harmony of goods – a totality in which there is a certain fitness between the contents of things and their designed ends? No entity can exist without relations of agreement (unity, harmonization) with other entities in its environment.[6] And there is a human sensibility that pleasantly experiences the proportions, fittings, conformities and unities of the world. The world, then, is constituted by beautiful agreements, and the arts – music, for instance – capture and re-express these agreements. But all of this, the whole classical legacy of beauty, Edwards names secondary, even inferior, beauty.[7] Thus, the theogonic myth (Hesiod) of the ordering (beautifying) of cosmos out of chaos, the intricate patterns of mathematics and geometry, even the awesome creations of poets, sculptors and musicians, are not beauty in its most original and authentic sense. What, then, is primary beauty?

It is just at this point that Edwards departs from the eighteenth-century subjective turn. By locating beauty in the 'dispositions of the heart, he participates in that turn'.[8] But here a subtle change takes place. For Dennis, Hume and others, beauty arises as an experience (a distinctive sensibility or discernment) that corresponds to pleasurable external properties. A certain ambiguity attends this correlational view that distributes beauty between human sensibility and external properties. But Edwards is quite clear as to what precisely and specifically *is* beautiful. What is primarily beautiful is not just an aesthetic sensibility that is evoked by external harmonies. Far more beautiful than that is 'consent, propensity and union of heart to being in general, which is immediately exercised in a general good will'.[9] Beauty, then, is not simply located in the human sensibility to beautiful things: it is, rather, the disposition of benevolence to whatever exists. A kind of beauty attends any and all dispositions of affection and goodwill – for example, benevolent dispositions towards family members, friends and companions – but, in these instances, the heart's feeling is evoked and shaped by particular circumstances and natural loyalties. More beautiful still is the heart that simply in itself and as such is disposed in benevolence to anything whatever. 'True virtue' is Edwards' term for this universal disposition, this consent, agreement and harmony with simply being itself. True virtue or benevolence to being in general is primary beauty – beauty in its most original and primordial instance.

Beauty as Community

Primary beauty is an unrestricted benevolence of a generous heart. But it has a dimension that carries it beyond mere subjectivity. True virtue is disposed towards the good of all things. As so disposed, it cannot but be attracted to, and have delight in, other beings (hearts) that exercise benevolence. Beauty, then, is the consent and harmony of the heart to all being, but a dimension of that beauty is the deeper union of mutually attracted benevolent hearts. This is of crucial importance on two counts. First, it is an expression of Edwards' theocentrism. That is, if true virtue as benevolence delights in the benevolence of others, it will be drawn to the primordial instance of benevolence, the lovely generosity of God. Second, it displays how and why primary and secondary beauty are related. Secondary beauty is the harmony, proportion and fitness into which the world is arranged. But Edwards resists a dualism that would posit two completely different and unrelated types of beauty. Primary beauty as a benevolent disposition is at the same time an 'agreement', a union or harmony with being in general, a way of being with all being. And, at the level of intelligent beings, this amounts to a mutual benevolence, mutual agreement and mutual delight.

The primary instance of these mutualities is God as triune. Thus the primordial instance and foundation of primary beauty is the eternal loving consent that constitutes the triune being of God.[10] The heartfelt mutual benevolence of human persons is founded in, and imitates, the benevolence that constitutes the very being of God. Further, the harmonies and agreements of the world order (secondary beauty) imitate or mirror the intersubjective harmony of mutual benevolence. This is not a panpsychism in which the ultimate constituents of the world are thought to be alive and thus capable of living mutuality. Edwards' metaphysics assumes a break between the orders of 'intelligence' and the inanimate. But some harmony and mutual agreement (and thus beauty) is necessary for there to be a world, and Edwards contends that the model for that is the intersubjective benevolent consent of God's triune being and, in an imitative way, the benevolent agreements of spiritual beings. Thus, nature, too, is a consent or agreement between beings. It is because the unities and harmonies of worldly entities do imitate the primary beauty of benevolence that human beings are not only attracted to the benevolent beauty of spiritual being but also to the secondary beauty of the world. Human beings thus can have a *sensus suavitas* that perceives that the 'naturalness of trees and vines are shadows of His beauty and loveliness'.[11]

Beauty and God

In the eighteenth-century English aesthetic, unlike the Hellenic and medieval approaches, God may or may not be connected with beauty. For some authors, such as Dennis and Hutcheson, a natural theology was part of the overall project. But, for the most part, the relocation of beauty into a human sensibility required neither a theology of the world nor a theological psychology. The new project of (poetic) criticism carried with it a secularization of beauty. At first glance, Edwards appears to be part of this secularizing turn. For, in Edwards, primary beauty is not an aesthetic sensibility but a moral disposition – in fact, *the* primordial disposition in which the ethical itself originates. Does this moralization of beauty dispense with God?[12]

However powerful the philosophical element in Edwards' writings, he always remained a theologian, an interpreter of matters of faith. God and the things of God were never far from anything he thought or wrote. We are thus tempted to grant to Edwards a theology of beauty that arises from the acknowledgment that the secondary beauty of the world is rooted in the divine creativity. This would not be incorrect but neither would it grasp Edwards' distinctive theology of beauty. Recall that, for Edwards, what is most beautiful is the heartfelt, benevolent and consenting disposition (which includes a relation of agreement) of a moral agent to being in general – in other words, true virtue. Primary beauty is thus something human agents experience immediately in themselves and in others. But human beings embody and act out this disposition only as it is mixed with finite limitation and the disastrous effects of sin. Human beings no longer possess the original righteousness of Eden, 'the moral rectitude of heart and disposition', the unambiguous divine-like propensity for good.[13] Yet, there is a primordial and unambiguous instance of the disposition toward the good as such, the disposition of love for being as such, and that is the holiness of God, 'the beauty and sweetness of the divine nature'.[14] In the classical and medieval aesthetic, beauty can be ascribed to God because God is the pre-eminent instance, the source and explanation, of all mundane goods. God, then, is the primordial instance of what appears in creation as proportion, unity and harmony. But for Edwards, we fail to grasp God's holiness when we permit God's metaphysical attributes of power, omnipotence, unity or eternality to define it. God's holiness is the primary and distinctive divine attribute – namely, God's moral agency. It is just God's moral disposition, God's consent to being as such, that makes God's power lovely.

It is implied here that there is nothing beautiful, nothing distinctively divine, about power in itself. Furthermore, unity, proportion and order, even as analogies of divine being, are only secondarily beautiful. Edwards does occasionally use the term 'proportion' when he discusses primary beauty, but the proportion is between the affections (the heart) and its objects. It is the right relation, agreement or consent of the heart to being in general. In this sense, God's holiness is what defines God's beauty. But what is beautiful is the lovely disposition to love, secure the good of, or consent to the being of all things.

The Problem of Objectivity

Clearly, for Edwards, primary beauty – both divine and human – is the heart-felt benevolent consent to being in general. Can we say, then, that Edwards has resolved the eighteenth-century ambiguity of where beauty is located – that is, it is simply on the side of human subjectivity?[15] It is certainly his view that primary beauty's location is the order of the personal: intelligent or spiritual beings, the mind, the heart, the affections. But is primary beauty absent in objects and in objectivity? Clearly, secondary beauty has to do with a property of objects. Does this leave Edwards with the duality of a 'subjective' beauty of the heart and an 'objective' beauty of things? Is Edwards' placement of beauty in the moral order and in the heart a 'subjectivism'? It would seem not. For Edwards, benevolence is not so much a feeling as a relation. Beauty is reduced neither to a sensation (the view that Hume and others opposed) nor to a pleasurable sensibility. As a consent, agreement, or even as a conformity, beauty is a way of being engaged with the divine being, with other benevolent dispositions in a community of benevolence and (consensually) with the total world order. What is primordially beautiful is the eternally triune, mutually loving God who, in benevolence, communicates itself to the world. Mirroring this triune primordial beauty, whose consent engenders the world order, is the created spiritual order (at least as ideally intended) whose setting is the secondarily beautiful world order. Accordingly, the theological, intersubjective and worldly elements in Edwards' analysis prevent any reduction of beauty to experience, feeling or isolated subjectivity.

On the other hand, Edwards is not an 'objectivist' if that means that he sees beauty simply as a property (for instance, proportion) of things. Primary beauty is 'objective' in the sense that it is an actual state of affairs, the primary attribute of God, and the deep relation constituting spiritual beings which is imitated by the world. It is 'subjective' in the sense that what is beautiful is the heartfelt disposition, relation and consent on the part of God as a spiritual being. Edwards' analysis (metaphysics) has thus undermined and transcended the conventional duality of the subject and the object. In primary beauty the deepest objective constitution of God and human beings coincides with a self-transcending disposition. Beauty is at the same time subjective and objective, both being and sensibility.

Beauty and Self-transcendence

The eighteenth-century English psychological turn was also an account of beauty's role in human self-transcendence. The complex and non-reductionist psychologies of Locke and Hume were at the same time descriptions of the various powers and faculties (sensations, the understanding, the imagination, sensibilities) through which human beings transcended causal, mechanistic or conceptual (rationalistic) determinations. And in many of these eighteenth-century texts, beauty and the sublime are powerful self-transcending sensibilities. For in the sensibility, where beauty resides and which correlates to beautiful things, the human being is never merely a package of bodily sensations or a thinking machine, but a self-transcending aesthetic sensibility.

Similarly, Edwards' theology of beauty portrays beauty as a power of self-transcendence. But his account sharply departs both from the English texts and their themes of taste and the sublime and from the philosophies of self-transcendence. Taste and the sublime are part of the new problematic of beauty because nature, the human face or the arts are assumed to be beauty's primary referents. When that is the case, the motif of beauty is restricted to a distinctive human sensibility that must be contrasted to, and held in isolation from, the ethical and the religious. The English authors would have great difficulty seeing the *imago Dei*, sin or redemption as aesthetic issues. In Edwards' theology of beauty, these contrasts and isolations are set aside. The English version of aesthetic self-transcendence primarily pertains to what Edwards regarded as secondary beauty. But if primary beauty is heartfelt benevolence to being in general, beauty is not simply one of various human powers, faculties or sensibilities, it is the deepest and most central way in which the human being is transcendently engaged beyond itself. It is just this engagement, the benevolent disposition towards the good of all things, that constitutes the triune being of God Godself, the 'original righteousness' of Eden, which is corrupted by human sin, and the compassionate life of true virtue. Being as benevolence, then, is self-transcendence, not merely as a discernment of the pleasing harmonies that constitute the world but as a heartfelt disposition and agreement towards all things – an attraction to the beauty (benevolence) of God, and a delight in the beauty (benevolence) of others. In Edwards, primary beauty as benevolence describes human self-transcendence not only of immanent, psychological self-orientations or of external determinations, but of the hold of evil. In benevolence primary beauty and the moral (true virtue) coincide.

In this respect, Edwards may be closer to the nineteenth- and twentieth-century philosophies of human self-transcendence than to his eighteenth-century peers. Yet, at a crucial point, his interpretation cannot be fitted into post-eighteenth-century ways of understanding self-transcendence. For most of these philosophers, transcendence is towards and into nature (and judgement), the ideas of things and the graceful body. Immanence, then, is some form of pre- or non-world engagement. But, for Edwards, immanence is a form of autonomy, the enclosed and hardened heart, and transcendence is a redemption of the heart that turns it to a loving, accepting consent of all things.

Edwards, thus, is a kind of bridge between modern philosophies of self-transcendence and theological anthropology.

Notes

1   William Shakespeare, *The Two Gentlemen of Verona*, Act IV, Sc. II.
2   Umberto Eco, *The Aesthetics of Thomas Aquinas*, trans. H. Bradin (Cambridge, MA: Harvard University Press, 1988), p. 10.
3   Jonathan Edwards, *The Nature of True Virtue* (1765) (Ann Arbor: University of Minnesota Press, 1960), p. 38.
4   The theme of beauty occurs throughout Edwards' writings. See especially his 'Notes on the Mind'; 'Images or Shadows of Divine Things'; 'Miscellanies' (Edwards' notebooks); 'Dissertation Concerning the End for Which God Created the World'; *Treatise Concerning the Religious Affections*, ed. John E. Smith (New Haven, CT: Yale University Press, 1959), Parts III, III, X. Edwards' most detailed treatment of beauty is to be found in *The Nature of True Virtue*.
        The fullest exposition of Edwards on beauty remains Roland André DeLattre, *Beauty and Sensibility in the Thought of Jonathan Edwards* (New Haven and London: Yale University Press, 1968). But see also Terrence Erdt, *Jonathan Edwards: Art and the Sense of the Heart* (Amherst, MA: University of Massachusetts Press, 1980), and Douglas J. Elwood, *The Philosophical Theology of Jonathan Edwards* (New York: Columbia University Press, 1960).
5   According to Terrence Erdt, Edwards adopted the framework of the Lockean psychology but added a missing element, the 'sense of the heart': *Jonathan Edwards*, Chapter 2.
6   'There is symmetry and beauty in God's workmanship. The natural body, which God hath made, consists of many members; and all are in a beautiful proportion': *Treatise Concerning the Religious Affections*, p. 292.
7   *The Nature of True Virtue*, Chapter III. See DeLattre, *Beauty and Sensibility*, pp. 192–96. Edwards cites Francis Hutcheson's work on beauty (1725) as 'uniformity in the midst of variety' as an example of secondary beauty: *True Virtue*, p. 25.
8   'If it [true virtue] has its seat in the heart, and is the general goodness and beauty of the disposition and its exercise, ... what can it consist in, but a consent and good will to being in general': *True Virtue*, pp. 3–4.
9   Ibid., p. 3.
10 For Edwards on the trinity see 'An Unpublished Essay of *Edwards on the Trinity*', ed. G.P. Fisher (New York, 1903). See also Delattre, *Beauty and Sensibility*, pp. 148–61 and 170–73. Delattre quotes Edwards, 'One alone cannot be excellent' or beautiful 'inasmuch as in such case there can be no consent' (p. 94). Then Delattre adds, 'On this platform Edwards erects his ontological doctrine of the Trinity' (p. 18). Thus Edwards can speak of Jesus, the Son, as the object of 'infinite consent' and the Spirit as the 'act of God between the Father and the Son infinitely loving and delighting in each other' (p. 149).
11 Terrence Erdt, *Jonathan Edwards*, p. 50.
12 Jonathan Edwards, *Original Sin*, ed. C.A. Holbrook (New Haven, CT: Yale University Press, 1970), Part II, Chapter I, Section I.
13 *Religious Affections*, p. 129.
14 Delattre, *Beauty and Sensibility*, p. 131.
15 Roland Delattre struggles with the problem of objectivity throughout his book on Edwards. If his work has a single thesis, it is probably that Edwards has an objectivist notion of beauty. Accordingly, he says that 'Edwards' conception of beauty will be shown to be primarily objective, structural, and related rather than subjective, emotional, and relativist' (ibid., p. 4). Delattre's development of this thesis is not without its obscurities. He acknowledges that primary beauty is the 'cordial or heart-felt consent of being to being' (p. 17). In Edwards' own language, true virtue is 'a benevolent disposition of the heart'. This is what is beautiful. Delattre can also speak of beauty as a 'passion' for seeing things

as they are and responding accordingly. But on the 'objective' side, Delattre says that beauty is an 'objective relation among beings' (p. 60), and a 'conformity to God' (p. 69). Perpetuating ambiguity, he says that 'disposition or affections of the heart' are 'involved in consent' (p. 17) and that the mark of beauty is the beautifying, 'that which has the power to consent to being'. In my view, many of these statements are misleading. To say that beauty is a 'relation among beings' and a 'conformity to God' can, without the location of beauty in the benevolent heart, be simply secondary beauty. And what is itself primarily beautiful is the disposition of consent itself, not a 'power' to consent. One can agree with Delattre that Edwards' view is not a mere subjectivism, that a metaphysics and theology of God anchor and exemplify primary beauty. That is perhaps the main point. But he sometimes makes that point in ways that turn heart, consent and disposition into objective relations.

Chapter 5

Beauty in Human Self-transcendence

. . . Thus beauty may
Pierce through mists that worldly commerce brings,
Imagination's blindness wash away,
And – bird at daybreak – lend the spirit wings. (Walter de la Mare)[1]

. . . Lord, I do fear
Thou'st made the world too beautiful this year;
My soul is all but out of me, – let fall
No burning leaf; prithee, let no bird call. (Edna Saint Vincent Millay)[2]

All things appear more beautiful, the more we are conscious merely of them, and
the less we are conscious of ourselves. (Arthur Schopenhauer)[3]

In the pre-Enlightenment West, beauty comes with being. For eighteenth-century English authors, beauty is distributed between a human sensibility and certain properties of objects. Throughout the whole period beauty is never treated as simply a utility, a mere expression of human autonomy. The nine muses, the manifest marvels of nature, the high arts, the human face and body and the splendour of God are never merely subject to human control, tamed to human agendas. If beauty pleases simply as 'being seen' (*visum*), it has a certain power over perception and experience. It draws the human being out of its immanence into self-transcendence.

Even if the ancient texts do not have an explicit term for human self-transcendence, they nevertheless offer eloquent testimonies to ways in which human beings surpass their own immanence. A jealous God of the covenant can confront and negate the human lust for power. A Dionysian ecstatic power can seize seers and cultic celebrants. *Gnosis* and a perception of the ideas of things can draw the human being above its subjection to the 'lower powers' of the soul. The 'sense of beauty', standards of taste and the sublime are eighteenth-century ways of portraying how human beings can be drawn to something beyond themselves. To experience beauty is to be engaged with something other than one's own desires.

In the eighteenth century, a new problematic was stirring the philosophical mood of England and Europe. Made possible by both Renaissance humanism and the Cartesian attempt to preserve the human being against complete reduction to the quantitative, the task of the new problematic was a comprehensive and systematic inquiry into the emotional, cognitive, moral and social dimensions of the human being itself. Locke, Hume, Malebranche, Edwards, Kant and the German idealists launched the project of philosophical (psychological) anthropology which was simultaneously an exploration of human self-transcendence. These authors exposed the ways in which the natural sciences (and all quantitative, external concepts) rested on subjective accomplishments – or, to put the point less idealistically, how objective knowledge took place only in connection with already formed temporal, linguistic, embodied and emotional structures of human experience.

In the long history of Western philosophical anthropology, beauty makes only sporadic appearances. From Locke to Heidegger, most of the accounts of human subjectivity, world engagement and intersubjectivity pay little attention to beauty. Many things contribute to beauty's low profile in post-medieval philosophies of the human being: secularization, anti-metaphysical and anti-speculative modes of thought and the ambiguities and obscurities of the eighteenth-century aesthetic. I shall explore the relation between beauty and self-transcendence by studying the difference between selected versions of self-transcendence that ignore beauty (Kierkegaard, Husserl, Levinas) and those that contend beauty is intrinsic to human self-transcendence (Kant, Schopenhauer, Desmond). A second issue emerges when we compare philosophical and theological anthropologies and, in Chapter 6, I shall look to Jonathan Edwards for help in framing this issue. Both of these issues, beauty's presence or absence in human self-transcendence, and a theological dimension of self-transcendence, are crucial for this work's central topic – beauty's place in the life of faith.

Human Self-transcendence without Beauty

Chapters 2 through 5 of this work review certain high points in the Western tale of beauty – texts that can serve as resources for a theological aesthetic. We come now to a fourth moment in that story, beauty as an intrinsic feature of human self-transcendence in modern nineteenth- and twentieth-century philosophical anthropologies. To illustrate interpretations of human self-transcendence I shall use three quite different philosophical texts that more or less ignore beauty: Søren Kierkegaard, the Danish philosopher–theologian who influenced existential departures from idealism; Edmund Husserl, the founder of the European phenomenological movement; and Emmanuel Levinas, the Jewish philosopher of the Sorbonne for whom self-transcendence and the ethical were interchangeable.

Self-transcendence as Passionate Subjectivity

Søren Kierkegaard's version of human self-transcendence confronts us with an ambiguous terminology and a mix of philosophical and theological elements. Like Kant and unlike Levinas, Kierkegaard understands self-transcendence by way of differentiated human dimensions.[4] His inquiry involves a double shift of autonomy into transcendence: first, from the aesthetic into the ethical; second, from the ethical into the religious where there is another double shift. However, we should not let Kierkegaard's terms, aesthetic and ethical, mislead us. The aesthetic is not an account of beauty or of artistic experience, nor is the ethical an account of moral consciousness. Rather, the aesthetic refers to something not very different from Schopenhauer's will – an everyday life that is driven by momentary desires and needs, in which the sense of being an existing, responsible subject has not yet arisen. In what Kierkegaard calls 'the aesthetic stage', the human being's situation and even very 'existence' remains concealed. There is no genuine inwardness, no existential self-consciousness, only a melancholy preoccupation with immediate satisfactions. The ethical marks a break with the aesthetic – a radical shift in which the human being becomes self-responsible and engaged with the task of being a subject. The ethical thus is passionate subjectivity, the passionate taking up of the task of being a subject, responsible for itself.

So far, Kierkegaard has conducted a philosophical reflection on the problem of immanence and autonomy. It is clear that the shift to the ethical is not a shift into the intersubjective and the world of the other. Unlike Buber, Marcel, Merleau-Ponty and others, Kierkegaard did not see the intersubjective as primary to subjectivity. Intersubjectivity arises only with a second and completely paradoxical shift into the religious, into faith. And if only an other, divine or human, can interrupt and challenge autonomy, then even Kierkegaard's ethical stage of passionate subjective is a form of autonomy. Duty calls to it, but this seems to be more an impersonal, categorical imperative than a genuine other. Thus, a second shift is called for and, with that shift into the religious, Kierkegaard leaves the philosophical behind and enters the world of faith which is related to the ethical (and philosophical) only in discontinuity, paradoxicality and the metaphor of the leap.

Does Kierkegaard's version of the route to transcendence leave us with a dichotomy between beauty and the ethical? We must take care again not to read Kierkegaard's aesthetic as beauty and his ethical as the moral life. We must also remind ourselves that these so-called stages are not so much sequential periods (as they were in his initial, youthful formulation) as typological terms for concurrent dimensions of life, each one of which can have specific cultural and individual expressions.[5] Thus, each stage can be taken up into, and transformed by, another stage. Accordingly, the ethical – the passionate subjectivity and self-responsible striving of the existing individual – takes up into itself what is prior to itself, the aesthetic.

This is not to say that beauty is completely absent in Kierkegaard's account of the relation between the aesthetic and the ethical.[6] The issue that concerns him is how, and under what conditions, authentic beauty arises in human life. He is clear that it does not come with the aesthetic stage. At this point Kierkegaard is strongly critical of the traditional dichotomy between the aesthetic and the ethical – a dichotomy he attributes to the aesthetic point of view and the notion of beauty that accompanies it. For the aesthete, beauty is what has its teleology in itself (like arts for art's sake). Thus, because aesthetes focus on individual beautiful entities and how they fulfil experience, they must empty beauty of everything negative. For the aesthete, the young girl is beautiful but never the ageing woman. Beauty comes with leisurely pleasure, not the ordinary toils of everyday life. All this is changed by the ethical. From the ethical point of view, the aesthete is not engaged with authentic beauty because the aesthete is too self-preoccupied, not yet being an existing human being, to discern true beauty. That discernment requires the passionate and responsible existence of the ethical. Ethical orientation thus finds a 'higher beauty' everywhere: in the dignity of human work, in the aged, in what shows sadness and loss. Kierkegaard does, then, maintain that (ethical) self-transcendence is the necessary condition of the discernment of beauty, and this enables him to oppose any view that locates beauty only in the aesthetic. What he does not do is discern a kind of beauty in this very self-transcendence – a beauty of the ethical itself. Rather, ethical self-transcendence is a necessary condition for the discernment of authentic beauty.

Self-transcendence as Intentional Meaning

'Philosophical anthropology' was not Edmund Husserl's primary concern. His project was to show why an objective knowledge of the world (as, for instance, in the sciences) was not undermined by its dependence on apparently subjective processes of consciousness. Nevertheless, one outcome of Husserl's project was the articulation of various ways in which human beings are self-transcending. The primary meaning of this self-transcendence was neither ethical nor religious. Neither the ethical (moral experience, obligation) nor the religious (relation to the sacred) could be possible if the human being did not surpass physical sensations and the immanent flow of psychological processes by being seized by something that transcends immanent activities. For Husserl this 'something' is the meaning-content of things that is not reducible to any conscious act or psychological state (*Erlebnis*). 'Meaning' here does not refer to that which stirs the emotions, as in 'That means a lot to me'. Rather, it is an objective, represented content (*Vorstellung*) which is not simply created by psychological motivations or agendas.[7] The human being is intrinsically incapable of simply willing that a sphere have the contents of a right angle. We may autonomously determine whether or not we want to think about a sphere or an angle, or whether we prefer spheres to angles, but we cannot autonomously think of a sphere *as* an angle, or a cat *as* a dog.

This is what led Husserl to his philosophy of intentionality: that insofar as meanings penetrate the retentions and protentions of time-consciousness, consciousness is never simply an internal set of sensations but is always already structurally drawn out of itself by and into the world. Accordingly, the human being does not determine the world out of itself, but loses its autonomy by being drawn out of pure immanence by meant entities that refuse to be utterly subject to the human will. Because of this inevitable and constant accedence to meanings and their contents that are irreducible to psychological phenomena, life in the everyday world is a perpetual transcendence. In the everyday world, the contents of meant things correspond to, and require, a certain type of meaning-act in the consciousness which does not itself produce these contents but must adapt itself to them – for example, to a melody, a certain physical shape, an abstract idea. In this way, the human being is not a mere prisoner to the flow of its own consciousness or a slave to its own self-interests, perspectives and agendas.

Self-transcendence as Radical Responsibility

Emmanuel Levinas's account of the genesis of the ethical exposes a major ambiguity of the term 'self-transcendence'. For what is the 'immanence' which transcending surpasses or goes beyond? When our primary fascination is with the rather astonishing phenomenon of human knowledge, the fact that human beings can make cognitive judgements about their world, immanence refers to the precognitive innocence of sensations, prejudices, organic drives and the like. To know is to transcend such things. In this view, transcendence concerns powers to name, seek evidences and critically assess past judgements. From Plato to Kant, Russell and Heidegger, Western philosophy has been enamoured with understanding, knowledge, revelation, argument, intuition, truth, science, unconcealing.

On the other hand, 'immanence' can refer to the human inability to move outside of its own passionate self-interests, to depart from its residence in a morally solipsistic world where only its own urges, needs and agendas are real. Reduced to such immanence, the human being, oblivious to the self-reality of the other, experiences no responsibility for the other. In the Kierkegaard texts, passionate subjectivity can transcend itself towards the genuine other only in a radically paradoxical act. Jean-Paul Sartre reformulated this Kierkegaardian view by arguing that the for-itself grasps the other only as what objectifies and nullifies itself. In this second sense, self-transcendence is not just a cognitive power of critical orientation but a break with the human being's existential and 'natural' autonomy. Self-transcendence, then, is a moral task, not just an epistemological curiosity. Both Kierkegaard (in his notion of ethical and religious stages) and Kant (in the second *Critique*) articulated self-transcendence in this sense. Behind both are centuries of a religious tradition whose notions of sin, Torah, virtue and redemption add up to a vision of human immanence as self-promoting, destructive autonomy and self-transcendence as a kind of (ethical) redemption.

Immanence and (ethical) self-transcendence constitute the primary themes of the philosophical project of Emmanuel Levinas.[8] Initially, Levinas seems to simply perpetuate Kierkegaard's polemic against the aesthetic. Both texts contain criticisms of totalizing thinking and argue the primacy of the ethical over the aesthetic. But Levinas's polemic shifts away from that of Kierkegaard. Kierkegaard was concerned with the devastating effects for religion, faith, ethics, philosophy, and even human society, of any and all thinking that is oblivious to passionate subjectivity and to all forms of life which eschew the task of being a subject. Immanence, at least as expressed in the second stage, referred to all the ways in which a society (or its religious interpreters) suppresses the task of self-responsible subjectivity.

In the Levinas texts the concern is not so much with *Existenz* (of individuals) as with a total society and epoch whose very structure permits, and even calls for, radical dehumanization and oppression. Recovering the ethical and celebrating passionate subjectivity still leaves the demonic possibilities of a totalizing society unnoticed. For Levinas, immanence and autonomy name not just the pre-existential narcissistic life of individuals but any and all discourses, philosophies, institutions and political powers in which the summons into responsibility for the other is absent. From Levinas's perspective to be drawn into meaning-contents (Husserl) is still immanence,[9] as are both Kant's pure and practical reason and Kierkegaard's ethical stage and passionate subjectivity, because the only genuine transcendence of immanence is by way of and into the life of the other. Moreover, adding a dollop of intersubjectivity does not help the case. Scheler's fellow-feeling, Heidegger's being-with, Sartre's look (*le regard*) all articulate immanence. Neither subjectivity nor intersubjectivity in themselves obtain to the ethical, for the ethical arises only with the summons out of all modes of autonomy. For Levinas there are only two things: immanence, and, responsibility for the other evoked by the other's vulnerability. This domination by the other's frailty and vulnerability defines what immanence is. As something not seized by the other's vulnerability, *eros* is immanence – that is, it serves autonomy, need and desire, not the other. The flow of sensible consciousness is immanence. Being grasped by world-originated meanings is immanence. Existence dominated by the task of self-responsibility is immanence. Ethics in the sense of a general categorical imperative, a biologically rooted propensity for cooperation or a societally founded system of oughts, is immanence. Among these figures of philosophy, Levinas articulates the most radical dichotomy between the ethical and the aesthetic.[10] Nevertheless, we should be clear that, for Levinas, immanence (and the aesthetic) is not merely evil, something to be ignored, overcome or suppressed. He can offer perceptive accounts of sensuous enjoyment and can even grant it a role in the opening up of the other.[11] But all of this remains prior to, and outside, the ethical. Beauty, then, has no intrinsic place in responsibility, in the ethical, or in life for the other.

I assemble these three texts, widely separated from each other in time, to illustrate a strand of Western philosophy that finds little or no place for beauty in whatever presses human beings to self-transcendence. Different as they are from each other, their accounts of self-transcendence need not be construed as exclusive proposals that cancel each other out. Each one portrays something about the human being that we ought not to ignore, and each one in its own way corrects the others. Husserl's analysis of self-transcending meaning-acts is the most formal of the three interpretations and, precisely because of this formalism, it is plausible to think that this self-transcendence is presupposed by the other two proposals. In the Husserlian view, all of Kierkegaard's stages require self-transcending meaning-activity. And it could be argued that the vulnerable other's summons into the ethical would not be possible if the human being were incapable of meaning-activity and of transcending what Kierkegaard calls the aesthetic stage. All three motifs together articulate dimensions of human self-transcendence. Yet, in none of these three accounts is beauty a part of what draws the human being beyond itself into time, meaning, passion or the world of the other. This omission of beauty from self-transcendence is not a trivial event in the Western tale of beauty. The power and influence of these interpretations of transcendence has surely contributed to the marginalization of beauty as a motif and to the conventional dualisms of the aesthetic and the ethical, and the religious and the ethical.

The Aesthetic Aspect of Self-transcendence

While the differences between the above three philosophers help us see different dimensions of human self-transcendence, there seems to be no place in these texts for beauty. There are, however, philosophers who do see beauty as intrinsic to human self-transcendence – namely, Immanuel Kant, Arthur Schopenhauer and William Desmond.

Beauty as a Transcendental Condition of Experience

Immanuel Kant's *The Critique of Judgment* is a landmark text in the history of the interpretation of beauty.[12] Published in 1790, it incorporated the major themes of the early eighteenth-century English thinkers – Kant had read Hume, Hutcheson and Burke – and rigorously elaborated a number of their ideas: beauty, taste, the sublime, the fitting (adaptation), harmony of form, and the triadic organization of human faculties.

If human beings had no capacity for self-transcendence, they would be mere fields of instinctual experience, utterly subject to external or internal causes, contributing nothing by way of initiative or creativity to their ongoing life. Because all three *Critiques* together describe ways in which human beings are not reducible to external causal explanation, they amount to an account of human self-transcendence. At the level of common-sense observation and immediate experience, there is a certain self-evidence that human beings experience things in nature, make judgements, grasp necessary principles and, in freedom, act beyond themselves in modes of responsibility. Kant's project, his 'Copernican revolution', was to discover the conditions that, in a necessary and *a priori* way, make possible these various territories of experience – cognitive accomplishments, moral responses and judgements. Without such 'transcendental' conditions of possibility, human beings could not grasp the world as spatial and temporal, sense moral imperatives, sense the entities of nature, arrive at concepts or make judgements. Accordingly, the transcendental structures set forth in the three *Critiques* describe how it is possible for the human being to be drawn forth into acts of knowledge, valuation, appraisal and obligation. Nor do these transcendental structures describe human autonomy or an absolutely sovereign will. In the sphere of theoretical knowledge (*Verstehen*), the human being does not simply will or invent the *a priori* principles: their inscription is there to be discovered. In the sphere of freedom and practical reason (*Vernunft*), the human being does not invent the imperative that summons it.

Kant treats the 'analytic of beauty' in the third *Critique, The Critique of Judgment*. Why was a third critique or 'analytic' necessary?[13] Kant had identified two human faculties: pure reason (*Verstehen*), the capacity for theoretical and *a priori* knowledge and for making judgements independent of experience; and practical reason, the capacity to experience and have practical wisdom in the situations of human desire and freedom. But something important is still missing in the analysis – in fact, the very thing in which the other two take place and which supplies them with the contents of the world. Not contained in either pure or practical reason is the capacity to cognitively grasp the things of nature and the way the experience of nature engenders the phenomenon of making judgements. It is just this third territory of principles and third faculty that links the other two to each other and which supplies the precognitive motivations that engender all acts of judgement.

Prior to, and presupposed by, both theoretical and practical reason is human life in, and engaged with, nature. Kant contends that something in this engagement originates human judgements and, in fact, the whole cognitive life of the human being.[14] Something is at work to provoke the very task of knowing and make the knowing of things important. That something arises with the human being's immediate engagement with the things of nature, the experience of the flow of contents in a world already there and given. The reason judgements come about is that pleasure or satisfaction (*Lust*) and pain or dissatisfaction (*Unlust*) always attend the human engagement with the things of nature. The human being is not a mere thinking machine. Prior to its thinking, and pressing it to think, is a world experienced by the emotions and the imagination as threatening, satisfying and problematic. Although there is a certain psychological self-evidence about this observation, Kant is pursuing something other than the psychological tone of human experience.

The pleasure or satisfaction that comes with the human engagement with nature has a transcendental element which necessarily attends the grasping of any and all entities in nature. To experience something in nature – a sunset, flower or stream – is first of all to grasp not sheer dispersion and chaos but a unity of some sort. However, it would be utterly impossible to grasp that unity if the human being were constitutionally incapable of experiencing or apprehending the way in which the entity is set in, functions in and is adapted to its environment. Thus, to experience an object is never simply to isolate it from its functions (fitness?) and relations. The capacity of grasping such relations is the condition of the possibility of experiencing any natural entity and, as such, is a transcendental structure of the human being. Kant's term for this transcendental principle is 'the formal purposiveness of nature'.[15]

Purposiveness (*Zweckmässigkeit*) is clearly neither a metaphysical nor a theological notion. As a non-metaphysical notion, it does not describe the *a priori* conditions or properties of being an object but rather a principle without which a sense object cannot be thought. As a non-theological notion, it makes no attempt to set the object in a larger, cosmic or theistic scheme. What links this transcendental analysis of nature to aesthetics is Kant's contention that this *a priori* principle of purposiveness is at the same time a feeling of pleasure. Purposiveness – the possibility of apprehending an object in its adaptation and fitness – is a positive, satisfying aspect of the everyday experience of any and all objects. By way of his transcendental analysis of the human being's relation to nature, Kant has elaborated the theme, so often found in the English authors, of aesthetic discernment or sensibility. In Kant's version this sensibility is rooted in the transcendental possibility of grasping any object at all. And it is the attraction of satisfying (or repulsion of dissatisfying) apprehensions of objects that prompts the human being to react to things by way of their importance, value or truth – in other words to make judgements.

Kant's analytic of the beautiful moves beyond simply his transcendental principle of purposiveness to an exploration of the beautiful itself.[16] Prior to actual aesthetic experience, and a condition of its possibility, is the pleasure at work in the transcendental condition of purposiveness. Kant follows Hume and others in denying that the experience of the beautiful is a mere sensation. Rather, the experience is located in the imagination and involves a reflective and imaginative response. He also follows them in saying that this response is unmotivated. Looking for what the beautiful object is 'good for' undermines the experience. What reflective perception mediates as beauty is 'the purposive harmony of the object', or 'the form of purposiveness of an object': thus, for instance, the play of dancing figures. It is because of this form that judgements of taste, judgements about the beautiful, are not reducible to for-me statements. To say 'That is beautiful' is always a universal claim, however much it is grounded in the transcendental subjectivity of the claimer. Thus, to say 'That rose is pleasing *to me*' is not a claim about beauty. What grounds the universality of the claim to beauty is the discerned, reflected upon 'form of the purposiveness of the object'.[17] And this form is grasped by contemplation which, because of the form, is plausible and satisfying.

Kant's attempt to stave off subjectivism in an analysis of judgements of taste is an important landmark in the history of aesthetics. But this argument pertains to beauty as it takes place in reflection, concepts and judgements. Perhaps more important is Kant's argument for the place of beauty at the very centre and foundation of human self-transcendence, the pleasure–pain engagement with the world. If Kant is right, the aesthetic element (beauty) is what primarily grounds, motivates and interrelates both theoretical knowledge and practical wisdom and ethics. Accordingly, beauty is intrinsic to the initial and foundational dimension of human self-transcendence. At the same time, we must note that, in Kant's formulation, it is possible to understand the faculty, territory, and even character, of the ethical without recourse to beauty.

Beyond Self-preoccupation through Beauty

In a time when so many earlier thinkers are 'rediscovered', one hears little of Arthur Schopenhauer. This is somewhat surprising given the fact that his work contains, or anticipates, a number of modern themes. For Edmund Husserl, self-transcendence marked the everyday life of human beings as they were drawn into the objective contents of meanings. Because Husserl's initial project (it expanded in his later years) was to show how the sciences were grounded in the structure and activities of a world-engaging, intentional consciousness, he paid little attention to the problematic character (anxiety, pleasure) of everyday life. He would vindicate and confirm common-sense experience, but not expose its intrinsic pathos. Yet, it is just this pathos on which

Schopenhauer seizes. Reason and the sciences may perform their useful miracles, but they are always in service of the human being's day-to-day needs of safety, sustenance and comfort. But because they serve and confirm these things, the sciences offer little relief from the perpetual struggles and worries of everyday life. In Schopenhauer's view, everyday life is not simply something to cognitively ground but something to redeem, or at least liberate. Why is this the case? Sounding themes that suggest texts from Buddhism, Kierkegaard, Heidegger and Levinas, Schopenhauer contends that ordinary, everyday life is a mixture of struggle, utility, volition, self-preoccupation (subjectivity) and immediacy. Altogether, these elements add up to an intrinsic suffering and even a 'thraldom' or slavery. His inclusive term for this pathetic mix is the *will*.

To will means to strive for, and human striving begins in its inescapable rootedness in the needs of the living body. To be a human being is to be subject to the physical and chemical forces, the limitations and discomforts of bodily life.[18] Since to live at all involves unceasing struggle in a situation fraught with dangers, the human being is a 'concrete willing through and through', dominated by its 'need and misery'.[19] To live, we will things, obtain them, work to maintain and protect them, lose them and will them again. Everyday life, then, is an endless exchange of willing and attainment.[20]

Whatever else everyday life is, its predominant tone is that of the useful or the practical. This is why the human being is first of all a willing – a constant striving for solutions. Hence, in the environment of everyday life, practical striving sets the human being's primary relation to objects. Much has been made in late twentieth-century philosophy of the inadequacies of 'subject–object' thinking. In most cases, the concern is to overcome an epistemological dualism of the knowing self and its known objects. Schopenhauer's anti-dualism was not so much epistemological as existential. The subject–object relation is the utilitarian relation of anxious subjects to needed or threatening objects. Three consequences unfold from Schopenhauer's analysis of the primacy of the will. First, to strive and to will is to be self-preoccupied;[21] a kind of needy egocentrism and subjectivity dominates the world of everyday life. Second, what the self-preoccupied will focuses on as objects are immediate, practical presentations: the chair for sitting, the food for eating, the dawn for illuminating one's work activities. Third, this whole scene of self-preoccupied willing is one of suffering:[22] what preoccupies willing is always a lack, a threat, or even a dire possibility.

Even though pathos and 'thraldom' are intrinsic to everyday life, they do not have the final word. The pathos and thraldom of the self-preoccupied will can be transcended. When human beings process the world as a series of situations to be handled, or things to be used, they are 'soon finished with everything'.[23] They solve one problem and move on to another. They find food, avoid a certain danger and develop strategies for future problem-solving. But the world is not reducible to things-to-be-used. In a shift of attitude and perspective, human beings can become fascinated simply with the distinctive and irreducible reality or idea (*Vorstellung*) of things. Something in its very idea can seize the human being and evoke an act and relation of contemplation. When this happens, that something itself in its distinctive content moves into the foreground while the human being's practical agenda and self-preoccupation move into the background. Or, as Schopenhauer puts it, the idea is 'the adequate objectivity of the thing itself'.[24] As examples, Schopenhauer cites the still-life objects in a seventeenth-century Dutch painting. The utility of plate, vase and table is there, but the viewer, instead of being prompted to have a meal, is seized by each item as itself. The painter has helped the viewer imagine another relation to these things than mere usefulness.

Several themes attend Schopenhauer's thesis that the idea can draw the human being into a transcendence of the self-preoccupied will. First, to grasp the idea of things is a kind of knowledge. But it is neither the practical knowledge that attends problem-solving nor the theoretical knowledge (reason) of the sciences. It is a participative knowledge that comes only with a contemplation that allows the thing to be itself. Thus the object of this knowledge is the thing-in-itself, not in the sense of Kant's necessarily unknowable and elusive entity unshaped by transcendental structures of experience, but rather as what displays itself when it is not reduced to utility.[25] Second, the world of the idea is *objectivity* in its truest, most authentic sense. The subjectivity of self-preoccupation presides over all practical, problem-solving and world relations. But pure contemplation 'becomes absorbed entirely in its object'.[26] Third, when the human being is, by way of contemplation, grasped by the reality (idea), its subjectivity recedes. The thing as idea is no longer an object doing the cognitive bidding of a subject. It recedes as this kind of object even as the subject becomes will-less. That is, the self that urgently and anxiously wills to solve and dominate recedes before the thing-as-itself as idea.

Buber, Levinas and others have shown how the self recedes in an experience of a genuine other. Schopenhauer likewise contends that anything, grasped as idea, will effect this receding, but unlike them (and like Heidegger) he discovers in this self-transcendence an aesthetic dimension. For to grasp a thing as its idea is at the same time to confront something beautiful. Neither use nor neutral content would be sufficient to turn the self's preoccupation into will-less participation. Only beauty can perform that miracle. For beauty is the quality of the object that facilitates knowledge of its idea.[27] The aesthetic relation to things – that is, a relation to things as beautiful – takes place only when motivated self-concern recedes. As he says:

> The beauty of the objects of a landscape, which now delights us, would have vanished if we stood to them in personal relations of which we always remain conscious. Everything is beautiful only so long as it does not concern us.[28]

The arts have a special relation to beauty precisely because the artist has radically broken with the world of will as it is intensely focused on the idea, thus on beauty. And to enjoy works of art requires a similar will-less engagement with the ideas of things. This engagement is the condition both of producing and enjoying works of art and of 'the susceptibility to the beautiful and the sublime'.[29]

The human being can transcend itself as will, as reduced to its own self-preoccupied needs and useful world engagement. It can experience a liberation from the pathos (slavery) and objectivism of the everyday world when it contemplatively participates in the ideas (which is also to say, the beauty) of things. This liberation seems not to have an ethical character. Ethics and responsibility seem to fall on the side of the will, the need to organize and maintain the world for our good. The one possible ethical implication of Schopenhauer's aesthetic self-transcendence is that to grasp a human other as idea (thus as beautiful) is to refuse simply to use, manage or dominate it. In this sense the idea and beauty confront and restrict human autonomy.

The Beauty of the Graceful Body

For Kant, beauty arises as a necessary aspect of a transcendental condition (purposiveness) for apprehending the form of objects of nature. Schopenhauer moves the analysis away from the transcendental to a capacity for apprehending objects as ideas which, as such, are attractively beautiful. Both texts, accordingly, perpetuate the eighteenth-century argument that sensation alone does not mediate beauty (see, for instance, Hume). Instead, beauty arises with the imagination's reflective or contemplative engagement with things. However, if beauty or the sense of beauty is simply placed outside the senses, a whole dimension of human self-transcendence and of the location of beauty is simply passed over. One strand of late twentieth-century continental philosophy calls us back from dualisms of body and imagination and of sense experience and reflective discernment.

Twentieth-century continental philosophy has seen a variety of periods and movements: phenomenology, existentialism, post-structuralism, deconstruction, and critical and feminist philosophy. As offspring of Kant's critical philosophy, these movements all depart from universalizing, speculative and rationalistic metaphysics. If they are concerned with 'being' at all, they would approach it from the human–world relationship. Whatever else 'being' might be in itself, it is always a coming forth, an illumination, that precedes and grounds theoretical, factual and scientific modes of knowledge. It is the very phenomenon of world display that arises with that strange entity, the human being (*Dasein*). Accordingly, it is not surprising that continental philosophers, at least prior to the rise of the philosophies of deconstruction, were fascinated with the primordial world engagement of the human being: with life-world (Husserl), being-in-the-world (Heidegger), availability (Marcel), perception (Merleau-Ponty) and the social world (Schutz).

A recurring motif of these analyses of human world engagement is the concrete immediacy of the lived body.[30] And to understand the lived body is also to understand an important dimension of human self-transcendence. Like almost all twentieth-century philosophies, continental philosophy has tried to move beyond dualist ways of understanding human beings and how they relate to the world – dualisms of thought and extension, mind (or soul) and body, spirit and matter. Marcel, Merleau-Ponty, Ricoeur and many others worked to discredit the notion that we human beings simply 'have' bodies as if our body was some sort of external possession added on to our real being like a winter coat or as if we were ghosts that occupied and ran a physiological machine. When we move our arms, converse with others, or listen to a melody, we are not pulling levers and punching buttons *so that* we can do those things. The 'we' or 'I' is not some substance that runs the body like an operator of a crane but is, from the outset, embodied. The only self that we know is this embodied self. We are 'in' our environment by means of body relations involving place, space, organic needs, bodily performances and sense perceptions. Nor is this embodied way of being a term for a mere field of sensations or a machine-body that neutrally processes data. The embodiment that is the very immediacy of existing and living gathers together appetites and satisfactions. And there is nothing bloodless or neutral about this complex bodily life. Furthermore, even as human emotions, thought processes and experiences take place from and in the field of the body, so does the whole of our bodily life take place in dependence on, and engagement with, its physical environment, and that includes the general biosphere of various life-forms and relation to other human bodies. Bodily life is ever an interbodily life with others.

Why would this engaged, embodied, flesh and blood life of human beings have an aesthetic dimension? Why would being a body and embodied being-in-the-world have anything to do with beauty? William Desmond's book, *Philosophy and its Others* offers a detailed answer.[31] To carry out its various agendas in the world and with others, our bodily efforts are never merely inept, clumsy or bumbling. We learn to walk, run, play and caress. Specialized tasks such as sewing or playing a musical instrument require of us even more complex bodily activities. To perform the simplest of everyday bodily acts, we must solve a variety of spatial–physical problems. This solution involving bodily coordination is always a kind of gracefulness that displays a certain beauty. There is, in other words, a minimum gracefulness that attends any successful bodily operation. Since we ordinarily do not observe our own graceful activity, we may be more aware of bodily grace when we observe the spontaneous movements of animals: the lope of the deer, the blazing speed of the cheetah, the awesome acrobatics of the peregrine falcon.[32]

But something else draws beauty into human embodied life. Our bodily engagements with embodied others – animal life, nature and the places and things of our environment – is never merely bloodless, quantitative or neutral. It is awash with aims and agendas that give importance and value to what we do and relate to. All sorts of worldly things are important to us: home, persons, animals, colours, events, sounds, expected and unexpected happenings. And these things are never mere nothings, mere collections of chaos or instances of ugliness. Many of these things exist in graceful movements. They, too, have accomplished degrees of unity of form, continuity of aspects, fluid motions and creative differentiations. Because we are bodily engaged with them, we do not experience these things merely as formal data. Our bodies prevent us from mathematical reductions of what engages us. To sense and perceive at all is to grasp valued complexities, bodily accomplished aims, graceful movements. We apprehend – in a certain sense, our body apprehends – what is in our bodily environment not in attitudes of indifference but of alertness, appreciation and even positive pleasure. Vassar Miller, a twentieth-century poet, captures this dark bodily aesthetic: 'At Thy Word my mind may wander, but my bones worship beneath the dark waters of my blood.'[33] Remove the graceful, embodied movements and complex unities of life from us and our world and we remove the world itself. In this sense, to be as a flesh and blood embodied human being is to be beautiful and to have to do with beauty.

Summary

I have reviewed both non-aesthetic and aesthetic accounts of human self-transcendence. The aesthetic accounts resemble the great theory of beauty in one respect: they agree that beauty is irrepressible, not so much because it comes with cosmic being or world process but because it is a mark of human self-transcendence. According to Kant, Schopenhauer and Desmond, the human being is drawn out of its immanence and autonomy not just by way of critical knowledge, passionate subjectivity or ethical responsibility, but by beauty.

Chapters 2 through 5, if not a full and exact history, do single out high-lights of the Western story of beauty. In classical and medieval Christian texts, beauty, as the proportion and harmony required for anything to exist, comes with being itself. The eighteenth century's fascination was with the sense of beauty, the human facility sensitive to the harmonies of things. In the nineteenth and twentieth centuries, the philosophical project of articulating human self-transcendence sometimes excluded and sometimes included beauty. This story constitutes a Western tradition and legacy of beauty. It contains differing, though not necessarily exclusive, ways of saying that beauty is intrinsic to being, life and human experience. At the same time, it contains elements that make it easy for later generations to ignore beauty. Those who reject theology, metaphysics and philosophical cosmology will see beauty as sharing the same fate as the quaint theological foundationalisms of the Hellenic and medieval periods. If God is dead, so is beauty. And those who think that only the natural and social sciences or various types of linguistic inquiry engage in legitimate modes of cognitive discourse and thinking will easily dismiss beauty, both as a human sensibility and as a concomitant of human self-transcendence. In the next chapter I shall take up beauty's possible place in the life of faith. I shall, in other words, begin a theological inquiry. Rather than dismissing the four moments of the Western story of beauty, I shall attempt to show how each one offers important insights into a theological aesthetic. In other words, I shall try to show how beauty as being, as a sensibility and as a self-transcending benevolence is intrinsic to the life of faith.

Notes

1   Walter de la Mare, 'The Traveller', *Collected Poems* (London: Faber and Faber, 1979), p. 343.

2 Edna Saint Vincent Millay, 'God's World', *Collected Lyrics* (New York: Harper and Row, 1969), p. 25.

3 Arthur Schopenhauer, *The World as Will and Representation*, Vol. II, trans. E.F.J. Payne (Indian Hills, CO: Falcon Wings Press, 1978), p. 368.

4 On the aesthetic and the ethical in Kierkegaard, see 'Equilibrium between the Aesthetical and the Ethical', in *Either-Or: A Fragment of Life*, Vol. II, trans. David and Lillian Swenson (Princeton, NJ: Princeton University Press, 1944); *The Concluding Unscientific Postscript*, trans. David Swenson (Princeton, NJ: Princeton University Press, 1941), Chapter III, also pp. 226ff, 262–64, 288–89 and 347–49; and *Stages on Life's Way*, trans. H.V. and Edna Hong (Princeton, NJ: Princeton University Press, 1988), pp. 441–42, 460–68 and 474–77.

5 According to Niels Thulstrup, Kierkegaard's early journals listed four stages: the immediacy of childhood, awakening in boyhood, the romantic in which the harmonies of boyhood collapsed, and resignation and resolution. The entries are from *The Journal*, 17 January 1837. *Kierkegaard's Relation to Hegel*, trans. G.L. Steugen (Princeton, NJ: Princeton University Press, 1980), pp. 96–100.

6 For what may be Kierkegaard's most explicit statement on beauty, see 'Equilibrium between the Aesthetical and Ethical', in *Either-Or*.

7 For Husserl meaning, presentation (*Vorstellung*), and meaning-reference, see *Logical Investigations*, Vol. II, trans. J.N. Findlay (London: Routledge, Kegan Paul, 1970); Invest. I, Chap. I, #9; Invest. V. Chap. III; Invest. VI, Chap. I.

8 Passages that contrast the ethical to the many forms of immanence abound in Levinas's works. See *Otherwise than Being or Beyond Essence*, trans. A. Lingis (The Hague: Martinus Nijhoff, 1981), pp. 3–21; *Totality and Infinity*, trans. A. Lingis (Pittsburgh: Duquesne University Press, 1969), pp. 194–216, 299–302; *Ethics and Infinity* (Pittsburgh: Duquesne University Press, 1985), Chapters 3–7.

9 Levinas has a variety of terms that describe what he calls 'immanence': appearance, phenomenon, *Dasein*, meaning (*sens*), the order of thought or knowing, the 'there is', subjectivity, symmetry, and the same.

10 Beauty is only rarely mentioned in the Levinas texts. What follows is a rare sample. He is expounding the distinction between 'nudity' the intrinsic, unadorned frailty (of the face) that is 'disengaged from every form but having meaning by itself'. It is a kind of surplus over all *telos* or finality, that which makes anything not absorbable into its forms and relations. When we perceive any individual thing, that thing does not disappear in its form, but stands out. But beauty introduces 'a new finality, an internal finality, into this naked world'. This invites the task of disclosing the thing by finding for it 'a place in the whole by apperceiving its function or its beauty'. Science and art then clothe things with signification. They do not, then, concern themselves with the naked, frail entities themselves, the event of fact, or responsibility and the ethical: *Totality and Infinity*, p. 74.

11 Levinas, *Otherwise than Being*, pp. 72–74.

12 Immanual Kant, *Critique of Judgment*, trans. J.H. Bernard (New York: Hafner Publishing Co., 1966). For interpretations of this work and Kant's philosophy of beauty, see Arthur Schopenhauer, *The World as Will and Representation*, Appendix; Hans Georg Gadamer, 'The Relevance of the Beautiful', in *The Relevance of the Beautiful and Other Essays*, trans. N. Walker (Cambridge: Cambridge University Press, 1986), p. 20ff; and Herbert Marcuse, *Eros and Civilization: A Philosophical Inquiry into Freud* (Boston: Beacon Press, 1966), Chapter 9.

13 For Kant's explanation of how the three Analytics are related, and why a critique of judgement is called for, see *The Critique of Judgment*, 'Introduction', pp. III–IX.

14 It seems apparent at this point that Kant's sphere of 'judgement' and aesthetic immediacy function in his philosophy much like Plato's precognitive *eros* (desire), Locke's 'sensations' and 'reflections' and Husserl's precognitive life-world.

15 Kant, *The Critique of Judgment*, Introduction, #5.

16 Ibid., Book One, 'Analytic of the Beautiful', #6, #7, #17.

17 Ibid., Book One, #11.

18 Schopenhauer, *The World as Will and Representation*, Vol. I, p. 146.

19 Ibid., I., p. 312.

20   Ibid., I., p. 313.
21   Ibid., I., p. 368.
22   Ibid., I., p. 196.
23   Ibid., I., p. 187.
24   Ibid., I., p. 184.
25   Schopenhauer's themes of participative knowledge, the transcending of the subject–object structure, and the receding of subjectivity as contemplation grasps the thing itself, all anticipate Martin Heidegger's formulation of truth, thinking, language and 'unconcealment' (*aletheia*). See *What is Called Thinking* (New York: Harper and Row, 1968), Lectures II and III, and 'The Origin of the Work of Art', in *Poetry, Language, and Thought*, trans. A. Hofstadter (New York: Harper and Row, 1971), p. 51. Heidegger contends that thinking does not take place in relation to ideas. Schopenhauer would agree, since, in his view, 'idea' or representation (*Vorstellung*) is the entity itself as it simply comes forth. Schopenhauer's 'contemplation' and Heidegger's 'thinking' are very similar.
26   Schopenhauer, *The World as Will and Representation*, Vol. I, p. 185.
27   Ibid., I., p. 202.
28   Ibid., II., p. 324.
29   Ibid., I., p. 194.
30   A few of the major texts are the following. Maurice Merleau-Ponty, *The Phenomenology of Perception*, trans. C. Smith (London: Routledge and Kegan Paul, 1962), Part One; Gabriel Marcel, *The Mystery of Being*, Vol. I, trans. Rene Hague (London: Harvill Press), Chapter IV; and, 'Incarnate Being as the Central Datum of Metaphysical Reflection', in *Creative Fidelity*, trans. R. Rosenthal (New York: Farrar, Straus and Co., 1964), Chapter I; Jean-Paul Sartre, *Being and Nothingness*, trans. Hazel Barnes (New York: Philosophical Library, 1956), Part III; and Paul Ricoeur, *Freedom and Nature: The Voluntary and the Involuntary*, trans. E. Kohak (Evanston, IL: Northwestern University Press, 1966), Part I, Chapter 2. For an exposition of embodiment in Sartre, Marcel, and Merleau-Ponty, see Richard Zaner, *The Problem of Embodiment: Some Contributions to a Phenomenology of the Body* (The Hague: Nijhoff, 1964).
31   William Desmond, *Philosophy and its Others: Ways of Being and Mind* (Albany, NY: SUNY, 1990), Chapter 2.
32   John D. Barrow portrays the larger cosmic and evolutionary setting for the body's beauty, arguing that an aesthetic preference irreducible to individual taste and cultural relativity comes with evolutionary history itself. Thus, the early scenes of biological life (tropical savannahs, seasonal changes, rain and its effects, variant greens, open spaces) are all still at work in the deep bodily engagement with nature. Human aesthetic orientation arises from an adaptive response to these things, and the emotional responses of human beings are coloured and shaped by this legacy: *The Artful Universe* (Oxford: Clarendon Press, 1965), pp. 99–101.
33   Vassar Miller, 'My Bones Being Wiser', *If I Had Wheels or Love: Collected Poems of Vassar Miller* (Dallas, Texas: Southern Methodist University Press, 1991), p. 106.

Chapter 6

Paths to Beauty in Twentieth-century Theology

One who knows Hellenistic piety cannot doubt that it is dominated by the Eros motif and has, in principle, no room for the Agape motif. No less clearly, primitive Christianity is dominated by the Agape motif, and Eros is alien to it. (Anders Nygren)[1]

Eros is of a markedly aesthetic character. It is the beauty of the Divine that attracts the eye of the soul and sets its love in motion. (Anders Nygren)[2]

Chapter 1 depicted beauty's Cinderella status throughout the history of Christian tradition, its pieties and theologies. Through the centuries Christian theologians have related faith to almost everything: language, society, nature (ecology), science, the arts, politics, medicine and ethics, but not beauty. Beauty, including the discipline of aesthetics in the sense of a theory of beauty, has occupied an important place in at least some philosophies but has no such status in the history of Christian theology. Only occasionally in the history of Christian texts do faith, piety or theology insert themselves into the larger Western tale of beauty. At the same time, the motif of beauty is not entirely suppressed by the theologians. And even as ancient and modern Christian theologies have found articulation in an almost trackless variety of agendas, methods and paradigms, so we find among the theologians many paths to beauty as well as different rationales for opening the door of theology to beauty. Accordingly, in the face of this variety, it is important for any theology of beauty to pose the question how beauty enters theology in the first place. How and why does theology find its way to beauty?

The most indirect route is by way of the arts.[3] Christian churches, much like other religious communities, have always made use of architecture, fine costumes, icons, poetry, rhetoric and music for worship, teaching and, sometimes, even contemplation. And despite the postmodern excommunication of beauty from the arts, where there are arts, beauty is not far behind. Because beauty is being, it insinuates itself even into the suspicious and resistant religious consciousness. And when theology would interpret the proper place and use of the arts in piety and liturgy, it finds itself face-to-face with beauty. Yet, this preoccupation with the arts, important as it may be, is only an indirect route to a theology of beauty. When beauty enters theology through the legitimization and interpretation of the arts, its place in piety, as well as its relationship to God, creation or redemption, remains obscure.

The two other routes to beauty can be found in theological texts on beauty. In the first, beauty enters theology as an aspect of theology's (or faith's) larger setting, the world. In the second, it arises by way of the discovery that something in the world of faith itself is beautiful. Until now, this analysis has been primarily concerned with texts from the classical period through the nineteenth century. To illustrate these two theological paths to beauty, I offer brief accounts of a few scattered Catholic and Protestant texts on beauty in twentieth-century theology.

While the theme of beauty is largely absent from most of the monographs, large-scale systematic theologies, trends and schools of twentieth-century theology, a few Catholic (both Roman and Orthodox) and Protestant theologians have nevertheless addressed the issue. For some of these thinkers (for example, von Balthasar, William Dean and John Navone), beauty occupies a central place in their thought, while, for others (for example, Nebel, Jüngel and Pelikan) it enters theology only as something occasional, or as a motif under a cloud of theological suspicion. However, the several books, essays and passages on beauty in twentieth-century theology are too infrequent and too varied to permit a credible and clear typology of approaches, although, with the inevitable exceptions that always blur typological analyses, the texts do seem to fall roughly into Catholic and Protestant approaches. The Protestant texts (again, noting certain exceptions) share with each other an anti-Hellenic or anti-aesthetic iconoclasm. If the motif of beauty is permitted to cross the threshold of theology (or faith), it is only after extensive chastisement, warnings and marginalizations. For anti-aesthetic theologians, beauty must pay its dues: William Dean's *Coming To*, a work in process theology, being a clear exception.[4] In the twentieth-century Catholic texts, beauty tends to have a more positive status. Accordingly, I shall organize this very minimal study of beauty in twentieth-century theology into anti-aesthetic Protestant and aesthetic–theological Catholic approaches.

Anti-Aesthetic Protestant Approaches to Beauty

A few twentieth-century Protestant theologians take up the theme of beauty. In almost every case – Karl Barth is something of an exception – their theology of beauty is so highly qualified and so negative in tone that it turns out to be an anti-aesthetic. Furthermore, in most cases, the grounds of the anti-aesthetic is a historically constructed antithesis between the pre- or non-Christian Hellenic (and/or medieval) tradition and the prophetic, relativizing and transcendent faith of Christianity. Versions of this historical construction are present in the texts of Anders Nygren, Jaroslav Pelikan, Gerhard Nebel and Eberhard Jüngel.

Anders Nygren contends that, in the Hellenic (Platonic) scheme of things, beauty, Eros, and the divine are part of a single system of concepts. Eros is the soul's longing to obtain the 'supersensible world and its beauty', a 'love for the beautiful and the good' and 'man's way to the divine'.[5] It is the 'beauty of the Divine [that] attracts the idea of the soul'. The very function of beauty is to awaken the Eros or desire of the soul, drawing it beyond sensible beauty to the soul's true destiny – the knowledge of 'absolute Beauty'.[6]

And while the two concepts of Eros and Agape are related only by incompatibility and tension – as in St Paul's writings for instance – the whole patristic and medieval (read, Roman Catholic) tradition collapses the two into a unity.[7] Antithetical to this Hellenic and Catholic Christian tradition of beauty and Eros (compare the 'great theory of beauty') is Pauline and Lutheran Christianity. Here, Eros is a form of self-love which is a 'devilish perversion'.[8]

Nygren's *Agape and Eros* is primarily a historical work. It makes no positive proposals about beauty in the life of faith. At the same time, it is a systematizing historical work that constructs two separate houses, the house of Greece (with its controlling concept of Eros) and the house of Christianity (with its controlling concept of Agape). Since beauty is correlated with the attractive lure of the supersensible divine world, beauty occupies the Greek house. It goes without saying that the mythology, religion, cosmologies and metaphysics of ancient Hellenism can be historically differentiated from the semitically originated Christian movement. But, if all aspects of Hellenism are related to Christianity by mere antithesis, if every notion (insight) of that period – for instance, the 'great theory of beauty' – are reduced to a Hellenic mythotheological system, and if the idea of beauty is assigned to that system, that historical project becomes yet another rationale for a Christian and theological exclusion or indifference to beauty.

Jaroslav Pelikan takes up the theme of beauty in two essays of a work on 'the True, the Good and the Beautiful',[9] which together constitute both a negation and an affirmation of beauty. Pelikan uses the anti-aestheticism of Friedrich Nietzsche to engage and undermine both the religious aestheticism of medieval mysticism (Hildegard of Bingen) and the post-Kantian aestheticism of Schiller and Schleiermacher. The broad thesis of the book is that intellectualism, moralism, and aestheticism domesticate and corrupt the Holy as true, good and beautiful. Religious aestheticism, rooted in the Greek 'doctrine of the beautiful', tends to identify the Holy and the beautiful, and this identification becomes expressed in the use of the arts and symbols to reveal the Holy. Nietzsche, after an initial Wagnerian flirtation with aesthetics, exposes the idolatry of aestheticism in his notions of the dead god, the Over-man, and the demonic possibilities of religion.

Contrasted to aestheticism is a use of the arts (and beauty) that expresses the Nietzschean critique and protests beauty's domestication of the Holy. Pelikan's example is Bach. Because Bach sided with the common faith of ordinary people against the aesthetic sensibilities and critical ideals of the Enlightenment, in Bach's music we encounter the beauty of holiness, not the idolatrous notion of the holiness of beauty. Bach's themes are the praise of God bound up with the concept of the incarnate one and the transcendence of the Holy beyond all values. Pelikan's point, then, is that beauty can be related to the Holy only by an initial anti-aesthetic, anti-idolatrous limitation that repudiates any mediating or revelatory power of beauty itself. Nygren and Pelikan both construct an antithesis between Gospel, Christ and transcendence and Greek and Enlightenment aestheticism. Nygren seems to allow no place at all for beauty, having consigned it to the fleshpots of Eros, whereas Pelikan does find a way for beauty to survive and function within the Christian community, but one that seems to be completely limited to the arts and a confessional use of the arts. To go beyond that to affirm any role of beauty in faith itself is a step Pelikan would not take.

Gerhard Nebel offers us what may be the most detailed expression of a Reformed theology opposed to the Hellenic and Catholic tradition of beauty.[10] He introduces the subject with the usual Protestant cautions against the idolatry of the aesthetic. It would be misleading to say that beauty has a place in Nebel's overall theology. His monograph is, rather, a 'theology of beauty' whose primary task is to show why beauty has no such place. His approach resembles that of Nygren in that it constructs a historical and polemical antithesis between the aesthetic world of Hellas (and *mythos*) as beauty's setting and the vertical and iconoclastic world of Israel (and Yahweh). Nebel seems to regard the typology as universal and absolute, so that the Hellenic West serves as a universal paradigm for beauty's setting, features and power as they contrast to the Christ and revelation. Hellas displays two universal features of beauty: its historical situatedness and, a transhistorical aspect, which, mythically speaking is the 'appearance of the demonic'. Hellenic chthonic and Olympian religious movements manifest both of these aspects. Beauty, then, is set within the specific cultural world of the 'mythical God', the 'beautiful God', which, as an infinity present in the finite, can appropriately be expressed in form and structure. This world of the beautiful is a consistently tragic world, a mix (or dialectic) of the beautiful and the ugly, a world where the Titans, the powers of the demonic and of non-being, are always at work. This tragic world of immanent, divine energies and presences is specifically Greek but at the same time is always a human possibility. That same world – the seductive power of the demonic – lured the Israelites to depict Yahweh as a golden calf.[11] Hence, the world of beauty, the mix of myth and the demonic, is a world against which divine wrath is directed.

In complete contrast to this is Yahwism and the event and revelation of Jesus the Christ. Yahweh can only be related to the world of the beautiful by way of a break or 'tear' (*Riss*) effected by revelation. This new world of Israelite and Christian faith is a world of sin, vertical revelation and Messiah, and it poses a choice between the two powers – Yahweh or the demonic–mythical. Thus Nebel can say that 'in Israel the beautiful is superfluous', that the golden calf is Hellas in Israel, that the world of the New Testament is totally devoid of the beautiful, and that medieval Mariology recalls the old chthonic element of an earth-mother deity.[12] Is there, then, a place for beauty in faith or theology at all? Yes, there is, but not apparently in this world, in time, history, the present life of faith, or the Church. For beauty can be non-seductive and non-idolatrous only in Paradise and as something that comes with God's final and complete revealing.

Beauty has little or no place in **Eberhard Jüngel**'s massive and important theology of God and his other theological works.[13] At the same time, Jüngel gives us one of the most intricate and subtle essays on beauty in twentieth-century theology.[14] As we would expect, the 'great theory of beauty' as proportion does not set Jüngel's starting point or approach, although he does retain one of Thomas Aquinas's motifs, illumination (*claritas*). Nor does Jüngel follow those Protestant theologians who construct a historical typology of 'Athens' versus 'Jerusalem' to show an antithesis between beauty and revelation. A strong Protestant iconoclasm pervades the text but is carried out in a subtle dialectic. And his conclusion is not unlike other Protestant theologies for which beauty is a phenomenon of the fullness of time, postponed until God's full, eschatological revelation.

Distinctive, however, is Jüngel's way of arriving at this conclusion, for his method of treating beauty is not so much historical as phenomenological. Utilizing Kant, Schiller, Schopenhauer and other texts in German philosophical anthropology, he offers up a philosophical analysis of the finitude and pathos of beauty. Appearing in this phenomenological analysis are the eighteenth-century motif of a distinctive aesthetic perception and its object, the modern concern with the 'work of art', and a Heideggerian way of discovering the close relation between beauty and truth. Jüngel's phenomenology of beauty can be understood in five steps.

First, beauty and the non-beautiful are located anthropologically as one of the human being's 'elemental distinctions' or relations that determine the way in which God, self and world are interrelated. 'Moral relations' and 'religious relations' are examples of other elemental relations.[15] Second, beauty as a distinctive perception and a distinctive object always takes place in a larger framework of truth orientation, and beauty's perceptive act always interrupts – or transcends – that framework.[16] Third, the perception of beauty always grasps something specific as representing (or mediating) a totality or whole, which is why the experience of beauty stimulates a 'feeling for life'. Fourth, beauty's perceptive act (like truth's) always requires light. But it is at this point beauty obtains its autonomy – Jüngel does not quite say *hubris*. For, instead of simply partaking of the divinely rooted enlightening that is the condition of all finite knowledge, beauty's light is that of a self-present reality, an illumination from itself. Fifth, beauty as such makes a truth claim and all works of art, which for Jüngel seem to be the primary objects of beauty's perceptive act, are themselves concerned with truth. This seems to mean that, in this act, something of the world is always illuminated.

On the grounds of this complex phenomenology of beauty, Jüngel moves to a theology of beauty whose central thesis is that beauty as a finite, fallen part of the world's pathos can find its proper place only by way of eschatological fulfilment. The setting of the beautiful is not only created and finite being, but also the 'fallen world'. Thus, a 'twilight', 'passing away' and concealment always attend beauty.[17] For beauty is never simply truth itself, its light is never simply the divine light, and its reality is never truth itself but only the 'anticipation' and 'pre-appearance' of truth. Accordingly, beauty is not, and cannot be, God's truth and revelation. Beauty may perceive a totality, but that totality is always the transient, relative world horizon, not the one, true God. The one true revelation which takes place in the 'ugliness' of the crucified one surpasses and judges all philosophical anthropology and its expositions of the elements of human relations. This one, true revelation occurs in the one who for us was 'made sin'. It is this and only this which is the truth itself, able to judge and expose all transient and fallen reality. Beauty in its truth and fullness, beauty fully merged with truth, is thinkable, but only in connection with resurrection and *eschaton*, in which it loses its status as a twilight phenomenon (appearance).

With this point, it seems that Jüngel has constructed another traditional Protestant iconoclasm that posits an antithesis between the one, true revelation and all worldly structures, all anthropological powers and inclinations, including the divine imago as something utterly removed by sin. And yet, 'antithesis' is not quite appropriate to Jüngel's dialectic. He does say that beauty and art are 'dangerous competitors' with the Christian *kerygma*.[18] At the same time, they are 'welcome competitors' because 'in the beautiful appearance they anticipate that which faith has to declare', 'the hour of truth'.[19] And in the essay's final sentence, Jüngel rejects any *absolute* antithesis of beauty and revelation. However, whatever he means by his term, 'anticipate', it does not seem to be strong enough to justify an actual thematization or appropriation of beauty for the clarification of any theological motif of God, revelation, redemption or faith. For this reason and despite his dialectic, Jüngel is closer to Pelikan, Nebel and Nygren than to his own mentor, Karl Barth.

Protestant theologians who do address beauty resist any use of beauty to modify, supplant or interpret the Gospel or something about faith itself. For most of them, beauty is something against which the Christian Gospel is set. **Karl Barth** is an exception. While beauty does not occupy a major place in his *Church Dogmatics*, it is present as a minor motif attending a major doctrine.

Given the absence of the motif of beauty in traditional Reformed dogmatics and in twentieth-century Protestant theology, it is somewhat startling to discover a passage on beauty in Barth's dogmatics.[20] Like Nebel, Jüngel, Pelikan and other Protestant theologians who address beauty, Barth begins with the usual cautions. Beauty is not to be included 'in the main concepts of the doctrine of God', or in 'the divine essence itself'.[21] It is not a primary motif' in understanding the being of God but a 'subordinate and auxiliary idea'.[22] Why treat of beauty at all? Barth does find a biblical warrant (Psalm 104:11) but, in addition to that, a more systematic consideration opens his theology to beauty. This rationale jolts us almost as much as the fact that beauty is present in this Reformed text.

Why does Barth open his dogmatics to the theme of beauty? The answer is that he discovers something about the divine glory that requires beauty as its 'explanation'. Accordingly, Barth's way of including beauty in theology closely resembles the classical Catholic theologies in which God as creator is the primordial instance and the through-which of all finite goods. Thus, the world's beauty is a derived, dependent beauty that imitates the primordial beauty of God. But Barth does not take that route. Instead he turns away, momentarily, from his analyses of divine glory to the human response to God – a response that includes not only awe, gratitude and wonder but also 'joy, desire, pleasure, and the yearning for God'.[23] Something about God's self-revealing awakens in the human being not merely obedience and fear but joy and pleasure – something that justifies our having joy, desire, and pleasure towards Him' and which 'attracts us to this'.[24] This something is not God's power, infinity or eternity. In fact, it is not any specific divine attribute but rather the 'form of his glory'. And this form must be such that God's self-revealing glory attracts rather than repels, and evokes joy rather than indifference. God, then, is 'glorious in such a way that He radiates joy'. God's self-revealing must, in other words, be beautiful. In this way, beauty is an important, if secondary, theological motif. Without it, there would be no reason to think of the divine revealing as joyful, pleasurable, and therefore attractive.[25] And if beauty is the form of God's self-manifesting glory, it cannot but attend the trinity since God's self-manifestation is immanent and eternal in God's triune being.[26]

There seems, then, to be grounds for saying that beauty attends every dimension of the Gospel and every locus of Christian doctrine. For instance, if the beautiful (attractive) form of God's glory evokes joy, it would seem that beauty would come to reside in the joyful aspect of faith and in the love embodied in the community of faith. But Barth is content to limit his concern with beauty to a particular motif of his theology of God[27] and, because of this theocentric path to beauty and this restriction, he remains, somewhat paradoxically, within the classical Catholic theology of beauty. Beauty comes with God and God's glory, not with redemption or the *imago Dei*. But rather than root it in God as creator and ground of finite beauty, Barth sees beauty as whatever 'form' God's self-manifestation has that makes God the attractive joy of God's creatures. Thus, beauty arises in theology, not with creation but with revelation.

William Dean's *Coming To: A Theology of Beauty* is untypical of twentieth-century Protestant theologies of beauty on two counts.[28] First, beauty shapes the way Dean understands both religion and theology. Accordingly, beauty is neither an antithesis to faith or to the Christian tradition, nor an isolated motif attached to a particular doctrine. In this respect, Dean's work resembles that of Jonathan Edwards. Second, Dean works within the Whiteheadian trans-mutation of the classical tradition, so that his theology of beauty is not only positive and constructive but cosmological and metaphysical. While he finds little concern with beauty in most twentieth-century Christian theologies, he does think that a kind of aesthetics attended the playful moods of certain 1960s movements in such themes as the dancing God, games and festivities.

Instead of expounding Dean's total theology of beauty, I shall try to fathom the reason why beauty is an important motif in his way of understanding of the theological task, his path to and rationale for beauty in theology. Whitehead's philosophy provides his conceptual framework. Thus process ('coming to') is fundamental to all structure and all specific entities, and process is itself a kind of aesthetic experience because it takes place by way of a contrast or differentiation between a reception of the past (the inherited physical pole) and a present response. Because a certain adventurous satis-faction comes with creative resolution of past data, this differentiation is a value – in fact, the deepest, most intrinsic of all values. Triviality and chaos are two ways in which the aesthetic can be weakened, for both reduce the satisfaction that comes with resolved, differentiated process. Dean also follows Whitehead's lead in discerning a divine element in process.[29] If God is the ground of novelty, to experience the beauty of ever differentiating process is to experience God.

How does Dean move from the Whiteheadian speculative philosophy and its conceptual scheme to a theology of beauty? The first step is a (Whiteheadian) philosophy of religion. Religion is 'the public activity that enables aesthetic contrast', an acting-out of the contrast between the sacred and profane. When religion works for peace, opposes discrimination and violence, and works on behalf of the poor, it is publicly enacting a certain beauty. At the same time, religion can promote mere triviality by perpetuating old forms and by opposing vision and novelty. 'Theology' is 'the theoretical activity where aesthetic contrast is conceptually entertained'. And because its propositions evoke appearances that contrast with reality, it is a form of aesthetic inquiry. Theology, too, can be mere repetition, in which case it betrays its own aesthetic character. But as the theoretical aspect of religion's own aesthetic activity, theology can inquire into the way in which the major themes or doctrines of the religious community express the (aesthetic) 'coming to' of process and of the divine working: hence the themes of goodness, compassion, sensibility, good and evil, and God. We have, then, in Dean's theology of beauty a mediation of the Whiteheadian metaphysics to the activities of religion and the work of theology. Because beauty is intrinsic to all 'coming to', it is theology's most inclusive and pervasive concept.

Twentieth-century Catholic Theologies of Beauty

A constructed antithesis between the heritage of ancient Greece and, with that, beauty and aesthetics and the Christian faith opens the door to beauty in most twentieth-century Protestant theologies of beauty. If beauty does pertain to faith, it is only as a postponed beauty – something that comes with eschatological redemption.[30] But patristic and medieval Catholic theologies – both Eastern and Western – developed originally by way of engagement with that heritage. That Catholic Christianity broke with many of the features of the Greek mythical tradition and from Greek philosophies goes without saying. At the same time, Catholicism not only retained and perpetuated Greek poetry, rhetoric, plastic arts, architecture and sculpture, but also modes of thought that helped the Church express both divine and created beauty. Hence, twentieth-century Roman and Orthodox Catholic theologians do not work from a cultural or philosophical antithesis between the Hellenic and the Christian, and therefore rarely voice the anti-aesthetic suspicions of the Protestant theologians. There is, of course, a Catholic tradition of iconoclastic (apophatic) thinking, but its roots tend to be Christian Neo-Platonism (for example, Pseudo-Dionysius) which denies that God, as the through-which of all things, can ever be identical with that which it grounds – that is, the world, all finite goods and language.

Just as the antithesis of faith and beauty serves as a unifying theme of most of the Protestant approaches, so theocentrism creates family resemblances among the Catholic texts. There can be little doubt that Platonic, Neo-Platonic and Aristotelian natural theologies have contributed to Catholic theocentrism. Hence, throughout the history of Christian theology, the theology of God has served as the prevailing way in which beauty is discovered in the world of faith. If the world is beautiful, it is because God made it so, and, if that is the case, God must be the primordial instance of beauty. Of course, natural theology is not the route to beauty for the twentieth-century Catholic theologians, but they do agree that beauty finds its way into theology because God (or Spirit, trinity) is beautiful. Just as Karl Barth is an exception among the Protestant approaches, so Paul Evdokimov is an exception among the Catholic figures.[31]

Hans Urs von Balthasar, a Swiss Roman Catholic layperson (d. 1987) was one of the twentieth century's most prolific theologians. His works include translations of the writings of Paul Claudel, monographs on various Church fathers, interpretations of German philosophy and literature, and many volumes on theological themes.[32] His theological aesthetic was part of a planned trilogy whose principal parts were aesthetics, dramatics and logic. The 'dramatics' recorded the event of God's love in the history of Christ and the unfinished logic treated the 'truth' of the divine historical activity. The threefold project moves from theology's foundation (divine self-manifestation) through description (of Gospel) to rational confirmation. But it is the aesthetic, foundational part, *The Glory of the Lord* (*Herrlichkeit*) that engages theology's 'first word', the 'perception of the divine self-manifestation'.[33]

At first sight, von Balthasar's theological route to beauty closely resembles that of his fellow Basler, Karl Barth. Like Barth, von Balthasar is critical of 'aesthetic theology' as found in the works of Herder, Chateaubriand and 'romantic theology': that is, aesthetics in the mode of an autonomous science. Also, like Barth, von Balthasar refuses to grant beauty the status of a divine attribute, and is wary of allowing beauty to control theology and its foundation in revelation. At the same time, von Balthasar is severely critical of both the Protestant and Roman Catholic 'elimination of the aesthetic from theology'. The Protestant elimination stems from its total rejection of the legacy of Hellenism and the motif of contemplation, the result being a postponing of the aesthetic to something eschatological. It is important to note that, for von Balthasar, the term 'aesthetics' names not the arts or a theory of the arts, but beauty.

However, von Balthasar departs from Barth primarily in the way he permits beauty to seep into, and affect, every aspect of faith and Gospel. This expansion plus his many attending historical studies of beauty in Christian texts through the ages make *The Glory of the Lord* a twentieth-century theological monument to beauty. Von Balthasar sees theological aesthetics as the study of God's glory (*doxa*) – that is, the divine self-manifestation, the radiation of trinitarian love. Divine beauty is the manner in which God's goodness shares itself, the splendour (cf. Thomas Aquinas) of divine truth and the goodness that makes these things attractive. This would seem to place him closer to Barth than to Thomas Aquinas and the 'great theory of beauty' as proportion. He even calls beauty a manifest form. But Barth's phrase, beauty as the form of God's self-manifestation, is very formal, its only content being whatever there is about that manifestation that attracts and evokes joy. Von Balthasar, on the other hand, appropriates the concept of form from Thomas Aquinas and thus links it to the 'great theory' – form as the beautiful apprehended in harmony.[34]

Von Balthasar also takes a step beyond Thomas. Form as such is not so much beautiful in itself as a sign of a mystery and depth behind it. And what is the divine depth but the divine love? His analogy here is Aristotelian. Form is the ideal entelechy of a life-form: it is that which gives the life-form an orientation. Jesus' mode of existence, as attested in the Gospel, displays the true form of the human being, a beautiful and loveworthy mode of existence. It is just this fashioning of form, at least in human beings, in which spirit makes its appearance as a kind of eternal light of God shining through the human soul – the glory of the form of the Servant. Thus, beginning with the beauty of the divine self-manifestation and the radiation of the splendour of God, von Balthasar has found a way of discovering how that splendour determines, and reappears in, creation, history, incarnation, the human form and redemption. He can discover beauty in all these things precisely because beauty is not just the formal attractiveness of God's self-manifestation but form as spirit and a sign of the loving mystery of God which not only manifests itself but appears and is embodied in the incarnation, the Church and redemption.

In **John Navone**'s *Toward a Theology of Beauty* (1996), beauty has the most central and most pervasive place in all the twentieth-century Christian theologies of beauty.[35] It is thus difficult to discover a route to beauty in Navone's book because, for Navone, beauty, like truth and goodness, is self-evidently primordial, a feature of God, and therefore manifest in all God's activities and relations. Because beauty is coupled with truth and goodness and is therefore transcendental, Navone's work clearly follows the line of Thomist and medieval aesthetics. But there are features of his work that go beyond the Middle Ages. First, he picks up the notion (cf. Karl Barth and von Balthasar) that if God is beauty itself, then for God to reveal Godself and move beyond Godself into activity is to communicate beauty. But Navone does not limit revelation simply to Christ or incarnation. Revelation attends all God's expressive activities: creation, incarnation, even the human being as the divine image. Accordingly, all of God's activities are beautifying activities, and all the doctrines of Christian theology have to do with beauty.

Navone also retains the medieval motif of pleasure or delight that comes with the experience of beauty, but his elaboration of the theme suggests the influence of Barth. Like Barth, he says that beauty is that about God that attracts creatures and engages the human desire for happiness. Thus, there is a correlation between beauty and joy (happiness). And delight or joy is not just the response of creatures to God but is primordially present in God's very being. Beauty, he says, is God's eternal delight. At this point Navone both resembles, and also departs from, Jonathan Edwards. Like Edwards, he rejects the view that primary beauty is the *work*, the product, and thus primary beauty cannot be simply proportion or harmony. Thus he can speak of the original beauty 'of consciously knowing, loving subjects'. But what is beauty itself in Navone's view? What is it about God that attracts and engages human desire? Edwards has a clear answer. Primary beauty is the disposition of virtue or self-transcending benevolence, the inclination to consent to and pursue the good of other things. Navone agrees that God (especially as triune) is the instance of primary beauty, and that this beauty is not merely proportion. What it is, however, is 'God's eternal delight', which itself is the basis of the delightfulness of all creation. For Edwards self-transcending benevolence, not delight, is God's attracting beauty.

Patrick Sherry's *Spirit and Beauty* (1992) describes itself as an 'introduction to theological aesthetics'.[36] Like von Balthasar, Sherry regretfully reminds the reader of beauty's Cinderella status in theology, rooted especially in theology's fear of elitism and aestheticism. While Sherry's work reflects a wide range of historical inquiry from Plato and the Middle Ages to contemporary philosophy (Mothersill) and theology (Barth, Evdokimov), his approach is primarily shaped by his roots in the Catholic theological tradition. Hence, theology's first move is to discover the origin of beauty in the triune God. It is after this move that Sherry makes his own distinctive contribution to theological aesthetics – namely a focus on the Holy Spirit as the specific locus and mediator of beauty. He can agree with Barth and von Balthasar that beauty originates in God's triune being and self-relation, and that it is connected with God's glory, but to say that God is triune is simultaneously to say that God overflows Godself into activity, expression and presence. And this is why the Spirit is pivotal in a theology of beauty. For it is the Spirit that manifests that glory and carries out the divine activity in the sphere of creation. Hence, when Sherry takes up the question of the relation between God's beauty and earthly beauty, including human beauty, he can argue that it is the Spirit's work that *inspires* an imitation of the divine creativity in human beings. Imagination, wonder and creativity are all instantiations of beauty, and all occur through the work of the Spirit. While Sherry does not dwell on the problems of defining beauty, it appears that beauty itself is the wondrous harmony of things brought about by the Spirit's creativity or inspiration. Because of this focus on the Spirit's mediation of the divine glory, Sherry, like Navone, mediates beauty as harmony (the classical view) and beauty as self-transcending benevolence (Edwards).

Richard Viladesau's *Theological Aesthetics* may be the most multifaceted and inclusive approach to the subject among contemporary theologies of beauty.[37] 'Theological aesthetics' in this work refers not just to the problem of faith (or theology) and beauty but the way in which all three motifs of aesthetics (imagination and sensation, beauty and the arts) play out in the world of faith. Thus, the author refuses to separate the issue of the arts and the issue of beauty but works diligently to show their intrinsic interrelation in the world of faith. This is demonstrated in the book's structure, since every chapter begins with examples from the arts that display the aesthetic form of the issue in question. Accordingly, the work does offer a theology of beauty and extensive explorations of the way in which beauty attends the life of faith. The work is inclusive because it draws on both the classical and scholastic theology of beauty and the contemporary theology of revelation, conversion and the cross. Thus, God's intrinsic beauty and joy is the ultimate condition and end of all genuine desire and experience of beauty. Sounding not unlike Edwards, Viladesau contends, quite properly in my view, that revelation, the divine display and the evocation of Agapic love engages the natural drift of human beings towards beauty and both relativizes that drift (as an autonomous desire for beauty's pleasure) and 'sublates' it into Agape. Thus, unlike many of the Protestant theologians of beauty, he refuses to relate faith (Agape, revelation and conversion) and beauty as absolute contrasts. Beauty instead is an authentic, divinely-rooted human desire and, as such, can be taken up into faith. As he puts it, 'generous self-giving love for the needy other is nevertheless perceived by the eyes of faith as a (morally, spiritually) beautiful act in the "theo-drama" being created by God's artistry: an act that anticipates the escatological beauty of God's "Kingdom".'[38] Furthermore, Viladesau discovers the pathos of beauty in the Christian drama, the cross and the suffering of Jesus being part of this. For the beautiful act of self-giving love cannot avoid suffering. We have in this monograph a bringing together of traditional separations – of the ethical and religious with beauty, of asceticism and joy, of Catholic natural theology and Protestant theology's crucifixion, of beauty and the arts.

From Pseudo-Dionysius to the present, beauty is deeply interwoven into the piety and theology of Greek and Russian Orthodoxy. One of the fullest twentieth-century theologies of beauty in the Orthodox tradition is **Paul Evdokimov**'s *L'Art de l'Icône* (1972).[39] Evdokimov does not need to discover a way to beauty through the thickets of an anti-aesthetic religious community and its theologies. He can, instead, proceed to discern the aesthetic dimension of Orthodox piety and sacramentality. In Orthodoxy beauty enters theology neither by a natural theology of God as source of earthly beauty nor by a single theological motif such as revelation, Spirit or eschaton. Rather, beauty arises with the way in which salvation occurs and with the way in which the salvific community is sacramentally and liturgically constituted. Since Evdokimov's initial chapters expound scriptural, patristic and (Greek) orthodox sources, it initially seems as though his way to beauty is through historical analysis. But this procedure is less a foundationalist appeal to authorities as a display of how beauty is constituted in the life and reality of the *ecclesia* from the very outset. That life and reality is formed by and from Christ, 'the epiphany of the transcendent'. The locations of this epiphany are the mysterious and distinctive transactions of the Holy in the sacred spaces and times of the temple and the sacramental events and multiple symbols by which people participate in the divine energies set loose by Christ. All these motifs are gathered up in the 'visual theology' of the icon which offers an image of the invisible God and an instance of 'illumined glory'.[40] It is just this sacramentally and communally delivered image of the resurrected Christ that frees the Church from both idolatry and mythology. Evdokimov does appropriate the classical and Platonic notion of beauty as the splendour of truth – a splendour whose original instance is the trinity but which is mirrored in God's work of creation – but the beauty of creation is not a mere contrast to what happens in Christ and incarnation; all God's beautifying acts coalesce in Christ so that to experience and contemplate Christ is also to contemplate beauty.

The Western story of beauty has certain high points: beauty as being (proportion), sensibility, benevolence and self-transcendence. The twentieth-century theologians of beauty incorporate this story in a variety of ways. For some, the Western legacy is largely absent, or present only by negation. For others, the Western legacy continues, especially the Hellenic notion of beauty as proportion. Two issues especially persist in the twentieth-century Protestant and Catholic theologies of beauty. The first is an issue between the Catholic and at least some of the Protestant theologies – namely, the tension between the Protestant suspicion of the Catholic way of appropriating the Hellenic tradition and the Catholic placement of the Christian Gospel in the larger vision of God and being. At work in this opposition are the familiar quarrels about faith and reason, the status of philosophy, natural theology, God and being, the nature of the imago, and the status of Church tradition. In Paul Tillich's words, the tension is between Catholic inclusiveness (substance) and the Protestant principle.[41] Beauty, clearly, is one of the victims of these disputes. To state this issue more specifically, is beauty something so spoiled by human idolatry, so drawn into the sybaritic self that it (whatever 'it' is) must ever be exposed and postponed by faith, proclamation and theology? Is beauty simply an eschatological symbol, a phenomenon of prophetic postponement? Or is beauty sufficiently like truth, goodness, value or love that it comes with creation itself, has its roots in God, and is an intrinsic feature of any theological account of Christian faith and life?

A second issue concerns the way in which beauty is attached to theology. Does beauty arise first of all in a theology of God, in an account of the divine Trinity, or glory, or creation, or is it first manifest in the work and effects of redemption? Here we have an issue formed by disagreements between theocentric and anthropocentric theological methods. Evdokimov poses a more specific version of this issue. Is beauty always already available to theological reflection because it is embodied in the iconic, sacramental and liturgical life of the religious community? Is beauty first of all a phenomenon of sacramental mediation? The variety of answers to these questions in the twentieth-century theologies of beauty helps bring to awareness and to precision the question of theology's path to beauty, or how beauty appears in the life of faith.

Notes

1   Anders Nygren, *Agape and Eros*, trans. Philip S. Watson (Philadelphia: Westminster Press, 1953), p. 223.
2   Ibid., p. 237.
3   The last half of the twentieth century saw a number of works by historians and theologians on religion (or Christianity, theology) and the arts. While these works do not pretend to be theologies of beauty, they do sometimes address that theme. Accordingly, 'theological aesthetics' in the usual sense of aesthetics as a theory of the arts has found expression in a number of important works. See Walter Nathan, *Art and the Message of the Church* (Philadelphia: Westminster, 1961); John Dillenberger, *Theology of Artistic Sensibilities: Visual Arts and the Church* (New York: Crossroads, 1986); John Dixon, *Nature, Grace, and Art* (Chapel Hill, NC: University of North Carolina Press, 1964); Frank Burch Brown, *Religious Aesthetics: A Theological Study of Making and Meaning* (Princeton: NJ: Princeton University Press, 1989); Roger Hazleton, *A Theological Approach to Art* (Nashville: Abingdon Press, 1967); Nicholas Wolterstorff, *Art and Action: Toward a Christian Aesthetic* (Grand Rapids: Eerdmans, 1980) and *Works and Worlds of Art* (Oxford: Clarendon Press,

1980). In addition to these rather general theological aesthetics are a number of studies of religion and particular arts of music, literature, plastic arts and so on.

4   Two other works in aesthetics by Protestant thinkers clearly do not propound an anti-aesthetic antithesis between faith and beauty. James Martin's inquiry is more a historical survey of the relation between beauty and holiness (from Israel and classical Greece to the present) than it is a constructive theological statement about beauty: *Beauty and Holiness: The Dialogue Between Aesthetics and Religion* (Princeton, NJ: Princeton University Press, 1990). Frank Burch Brown's project, *Religious Aesthetics*, is not so much concerned with beauty (although he does not exclude it) as with the larger phenomenon of religion and the arts. See also Richard Harries, *Art and the Beauty of God: A Christian Understanding* (London: Mowbray, 1993). I do not include these two figures among the Protestant theologians of beauty because each one is primarily concerned with broader topics, and their texts do not address beauty in an extensive or constructive way.

5   Nygren, *Agape and Eros*, pp. 143, 175 and 177.

6   Ibid., p. 174.

7   According to Nygren, Methodius is never aware of the tension between the two concepts (ibid., p. 437) and St Augustine retains 'the Eros ladder' and considers that the Christian love for God is the same as the Platonic *Eros* (p. 466). Pseudo-Dionysius follows Proclus thus identifying God as the Beautiful with Eros, and Erigena continues the tradition by saying that God's beauty sets up a motion toward himself (p. 606), a view repeated by Dante (p. 618).

8   Ibid., p. 740.

9   Jaroslav Pelikan, *Fools for Christ: Essays on the True, the Good and the Beautiful* (Philadelphia: Muhlenberg Press, 1955), Chapters V and VI.

10 Gerhard Nebel, *Das Ereignis des Schönen* (Stuttgart, Ernst Klett, 1953). This work represents a shift from earlier writings sympathetic to classical Hellenic thought and culture. For a summary of Nebel's book, see Hans Urs von Balthasar, *The Glory of the Land: A Theological Aesthetic*, Vol. I, trans. E. Leiva-Merikasis (San Francisco: Ignatius Press, 1983), 'Introduction', #4.

11 Nebel, *Das Ereignis des Schönen*, p. 127.

12 Ibid., pp. 127, 141.

13 Eberhard Jüngel, *God as the Mystery of the World*, trans. D.J. Guder (Grand Rapids: Eerdmans, 1983).

14 Eberhard Jüngel, 'Even the Beautiful Must Die', *Theological Essays II*, trans. A. Neufeldt-Fast and J.B. Webster (Edinburgh: T. & T. Clarke, 1995).

15 Ibid., pp. 60–61.

16 Ibid., p. 63.

17 Ibid., pp. 75, 79.

18 Ibid., p. 81.

19 Ibid.

20 Karl Barth, *Church Dogmatics*, trans. T.H.L. Parker (Edinburgh: T. & T. Clarke, 1957), II, I, pp. 650–67.

21 Ibid., p. 652.

22 Ibid., p. 657.

23 Ibid., p. 655.

24 Ibid.

25 'God acts as the One who gives pleasure, creates desire and rewards with enjoyment. And he does it because He is pleasant, desirable, full of enjoyment, because first and last, He alone is that which is pleasant, desirable and full of enjoyment. God loves us as the One who is worthy of love as God. This is what we mean when we say God is beautiful' (ibid., p. 651). It would seem from this passage that God's beauty (desirability) would arise more with God's love or Agape than with his glory. Yet, for some reason, Barth treats beauty under the attributes of God's freedom rather than God's love.

26 As far as I know, Barth never made the text of Jonathan Edwards a project of serious study. The two texts agree in making God and the Trinity the primordial instance of beauty, but the agreement is only a formal one. Because of his concern to prevent dogmatics from

being captured by some external, philosophical aesthetic theory, Barth refuses to say what beauty actually is. Accordingly, his phrase that beauty is 'the form of (God's) glory', is relatively empty of meaning. Edwards, on the other hand, is quite willing to say what beauty is, and his definition seems to come not from an external aesthetic but from faith itself. What is most beautiful (primary beauty) is the self-transcending, benevolent disposition to lovingly consent to being as such. Beauty is the very Godness of God. Edwards would agree with Barth that beauty comes with God's glory holiness. But for Edwards God's holiness means God's disposition to bestow and grant being as such to what is not Godself.

27 At least one theologian in the family of Barth's theology picks up this motif of the beauty of God's self-revealing. According to Jürgen Moltmann, 'the beautiful in God is what makes us rejoice in him': *Theology of Play*, trans. A. Ulrich (New York: Harper and Row, 1971), p. 43. In this passage, Moltmann criticizes the excessive focus on God's dominion, interpreted in 'judicial and moral categories', a focus he would correct by way of the biblical notion of God's *doxa* or glory which evokes joy and rejoicing (pp. 39–45).

28 *Coming To: A Theological Aesthetic* (Philadelphia: Westminster Press, 1972). This work is the one, fully developed theology of beauty in the rather large literature of Whiteheadian or process theology. Dean is critical of the few attempts at a Whiteheadian aesthetic, sometimes on grounds of technical interpretation (as with John Cobb) and sometimes on grounds of reducing the Whiteheadian aesthetic to a philosophy of the arts (as with Donald Sherburne). See Chapter 3, and Appendix.

29 Ibid., Chapter 3.

30 The statement applies to the texts that address beauty. If we expanded the range of texts to include Protestant works on faith (religion, Church, theology) and the arts, the statement would have to be qualified.

31 I have selected four Catholic theologians of beauty: Hans Urs von Balthasar, John Navone, Patrick Sherry, and Paul Evdokimov (Orthodox). While each figure clearly works within and from the Catholic theological tradition, none of them simply restates the Thomist aesthetic of beauty. For an example of such a restatement, see Armand Maurer, *About Beauty: A Thomist Interpretation* (Houston: University of St Thomas, 1983).

32 For an introduction to the life and works of von Balthasar, see Louis Roberts, *The Theological Aesthetics of Hans Urs von Balthasar* (Washington, DC: Catholic University of America, 1987), Chapter I.

33 Hans Urs von Balthasar, *The Glory of the Lord*, Introduction. von Balthasar's theological aesthetics has attracted several major interpretations. See Louis Roberts, *The Theological Aesthetics*, especially Chapter 8; Jeffrey Kay, *Theological Aesthetics: The Role of Aesthetics in the Theological Method of Hans Urs von Balthasar* (Bern: H. Lang, 1975); John Riches (ed.), *The Analogy of Beauty: The Theology of Hans Urs von Balthasar* (Edinburgh: T. & T. Clarke, 1986); and Roland Chia, 'Theological Aesthetics or Aesthetic Theology: Some Reflections on the Theology of Hans Urs von Balthasar', *Scottish Journal of Theology*, **49** (1), (1996).

34 *Glory of the Lord*, Introduction, #7.

35 John Navone, *Toward a Theology of Beauty* (Collegeville, MINN: Liturgical Press, 1996).

36 Patrick Sherry, *Spirit and Beauty: An Introduction to Theological Aesthetics* (Oxford: Oxford University Press, 1992).

37 *Theological Aesthetics: God in Imagination, Beauty, and Art* (New York: Oxford University Press, 1999).

38 Ibid., p. 207

39 Paul Evdokimov, *L'Art de L'Icone: Théologie de la Beauté* (Paris: Desclée de Brouwer, 1970).

40 Ibid., p. 142.

41 Paul Tillich, *The Protestant Era*, trans. James L. Adams (Chicago: University of Chicago Press, 1948), Introduction, and Chapter XI.

Chapter 7

The Beauty of Human Redemption

And herein does very much consist that image of God wherein he made man . . . by which God distinguishes man from the beasts, viz. in those faculties and principles of nature, whereby he is capable of moral agency. (Jonathan Edwards)[1]

When God created man in His own image, He did so in order that man might reflect as fully as possible the divine beauty. (Armand Maurer)[2]

Now mark yet again the cruelty of the gods. There is no escape from them into sleep or madness, for they can pursue you into them with dreams. Indeed you are then most at their mercy. The nearest thing we have to a defense against them (but there is no real defense) is to be very wide awake and sober and hard at work, to hear no music, never to look at earth or sky, and (above all) to love no one. (C.S. Lewis)[3]

Beauty entered twentieth-century theologies in two quite different ways: first, in faith's engagement with the world (nature, society and the arts) and, second, as connected with some motif (doctrine) of Christian self-understanding. Pursuing the second way, twentieth-century theologians attended to beauty in scriptural texts, in the Church fathers and medieval doctors, in the icons, buildings and arts of the Church, and in such specific doctrines as God, Spirit, creation or Trinity. Each of these approaches reveals ways in which beauty is present in the Church community, its liturgies and its texts. At the same time, these theological paths to beauty pass over what seems to be a crucial issue – namely, whether and how beauty constitutes, or is present in, the life of faith itself. For it is quite possible to say that creation (nature) is beautiful, that God's creativity is beautifying, that the Trinity is the primordial exemplification of beauty, that true beauty will burst forth with the eschaton, and even that the community's sacramental, iconic life is beautiful, and still think of redemptive existence in primarily moral, forensic or pragmatic ways. One could still consider human evil, redemptive transformation and moral, spiritual life to have little to do with beauty.

The following axiom poses an additional consideration to these approaches: *Theology's route to beauty should be determined initially by the way in which beauty appears in the life of faith.* In this axiom, 'faith' is an inclusive term for the individual and social existence that comes about as the result of divine redemptive activity. The faith of first-century Christians does not mean a list of discrete beliefs expressible in doctrines, but rather an individual, interhuman and social existence affected by redemptive transformation. The axiom prompts us, then, to enquire whether and how beauty is part of a redemptive mode of existence. Creation, Jesus, God's self-revelation and the Trinity may express what specifically constitutes the world of faith and may describe the conditions or events that make redemptive transformation possible. But the quite valid convictions that God's creation is beautiful or that beauty attends inner Trinitarian relations do not tell us how and why beauty is intrinsic to redemptive transformation. Even if beauty is an element of natural theology or comes with a theological metaphysics of divine creation, it may still not be clear how and why it is present in the life of faith (or redemptive existence.) And theological motifs become abstract, speculative and theoretical when separated from the fact of redemptive transformation – the fact that redemption took place and still takes place. In some causal–inferential sense, it may be the case that without the triune God, created world, incarnated Word and the ecclesial community, redemption would never come about. But, in reality, these motifs are important as subjects of belief and proclamation only because redemption actually takes place. To repeat our question: granting that these various theological motifs attest to beauty, do not all of them presuppose the fact of redemptive transformation? And if redemptive transformation is devoid of beauty, will people of faith ever concern themselves with a beautiful creation or beautiful deity?

To ascertain beauty's place in the life of faith calls for a brief 'archaeology' of redemptive transformation. Redemptive existence, the actual salvific transformation of individual persons in their communities, necessarily presupposes two dimensions of existence, both of which have had a long history as doctrinal motifs. The one is the overwhelmingly powerful and all-pervasive historical phenomenon of human sin: human existence as it lives only for itself, enslaved in its anxious weakness, idolatrous tendencies and its victimizing oppressions. The fact of redemptive transformation (involving liberation, forgiveness, grace, creativity and sociopolitical transformation) presupposes and addresses radical and pervasive evil. Eden and the symbols of primordial innocence know nothing of redemptive existence. Only with the 'Fall', expulsion and Babel does redemption enter the story.

The second dimension and motif arises as the presupposition of both radical evil and the possibility of its remaking. Radical evil is not a phenomenon of water and stone, external causality or logical necessity, but of human flesh and blood and formal self-transcendence. All finite actualities are, of course, vulnerable to accident, illness and demise. Individual living things can fail to obtain the maturity proper to their species, and whole species can fall by the evolutionary wayside. But we hesitate to describe such vulnerabilities, departures or demises as radical (moral) evil. The survival-driven predatory behaviour of animal species is not driven by malice or greed. The very notion of (moral) evil connotes a departure from something that should not have been, that might have been otherwise, that is alien and destructive to its carrier or actor. Moral evil, then, is a failure, a deviation. But from what? The 'original' ideal or 'should have been' that lurks in all notions of human evil finds legendary expression in the old story of a primordially innocent creature made in the likeness of its maker. But human evil's presupposition of an 'original' innocence need not refer to an historical instance. It is a logical, even ontological, requirement without which the concept of 'evil' loses its meaning. If there is no ideal or primordial innocence in an ontological sense, evil simply coincides with being. As such, it is necessary, ontologically intrinsic and unredeemable. When that is the case, evil is in no sense a departure, a corruption or a poison, but is simply finitude itself. However, two unfortunate consequences unfold when evil and finitude are made to coincide. First, the criteria for determining what is and is not evil disappear. Second, there is no possibility of redemption from evil. Accordingly, if redemptive remaking in fact occurs, this presupposes, or refers back to, both a factual distortion (radical evil) and an original ideal that is able to be distorted. In the old theologies the original ideal was expounded as 'original righteousness' and 'the image of God'. Original righteousness serves to prevent the identification of evil and finitude. The image of God specifies the content of original righteousness as sharing in, or imitating, the righteousness of God. Since these two motifs together express both that which sin distorts and what redemption restores, they occupy the very structure of theological anthropology and soteriology. Sin (radical evil) and the primordial ideal would be structural necessities even if the mythopoeic notions of Eden, the 'Fall', and *imago Dei* had not been included in the biblical text. Thus, in addition to the exegesis and hermeneutics of biblical passages, the theological way of uncovering the content of redemption's presupposed dimensions (of sin and the ideal) is to trace what redemptive remaking implies about the distortion of sin and the human being's resemblance to God.[4]

What we discover when we scrutinize this implied resemblance, the presupposed restorable content, is that it has a primordial beauty. Because the *imago Dei* possesses primordial beauty, human evil is a fractured beauty, and redemptive remaking into a new, compassionate, self-transcendence is a restored beauty. In this way, beauty is intrinsic to the life of faith and trails along with all of faith's motifs. It is not simply something that impinges on people of faith from the proportions or harmonies of the created world. Such is the thesis we must now explore.

The Image of God as Self-transcendence

If beauty is being – displayed in the ongoing resolution of chaos and at work in every differentiation and every world engagement – it attends everything we are and do, and even on those pieties and theologies intent on rendering it invisible. Yet beauty can disappear not only as a theme of a society's discourse, but also from the inquiries, meditations and self-understandings of religious communities. At the same time, because beauty has already shaped the human ideal of the *imago Dei*, it is a hidden dimension of the world of faith that awaits discovery and articulation. Beauty-less ways of understanding faith and the Gospel await and call for re-enchantment. But how is such a discovery possible for Christian theology if beauty resides only in a lost ideal, an imago which we know only as a faint, distant, legendary memory? Beauty as being will emerge, but if that is theology's only rationale for an engagement with beauty, the theologian must first locate beauty outside of faith and the Gospel

and then restore it by means of some broader conceptuality. Such would be
our situation if the redemptive remaking of human beings had never actually
taken place. But if redemption is real, the faint ideal of the distant, elusive
imago reveals itself. As the presupposition of redemptive remaking, the imago
is not merely a shadowy refraction hidden in the detritus of human history.
For what redemption means is the transformation of evil's various unfreedoms
into new freedoms – new forms of formal and ethical self-transcendence.
Redemption exposes not only the horrifying, dehumanizing work of human
evil but also its ugliness. This exposure of the distorted ugliness of the human
being carries with it the presupposed beauty of the imago that evil distorts.
That redemption is actual and not merely possible, formal or theoretical is
what is proclaimed by the Gospel or good news. And it is through the three
motifs of *imago Dei*, unfreedom and redemption that beauty is displayed in
the world of faith and is accessible to theological inquiry.

Formal and Ethical Self-transcendence

What facets of the human being does sin distort and redemption restore? A
radical Barthianism might answer, 'Nothing whatsoever'. The 'image of God'
names a relation to God that only comes into existence with God's gracious
initiative. But what would be the aim of such an initiative? Is that, too, 'nothing
whatsoever'? Are we to say that redemption has no actual transformative
power at all, that it brings nothing about in the life of human individuals or
communities? It seems evident that an actual redemptive remaking presupposes
something that is remakable – something that is always already there. What
would that be? Any adequate answer to this question must meet two requirements; first, the presupposed structure must be something about the human
being which sin is able to distort and redemption transform; and, second, this
distortable and transformable something must be what bears a resemblance to
God.[5] Both requirements are fulfilled by human self-transcendence. Yet, as
soon as we say this, we confront once again the ambiguity of the expression,
'self-transcendence'. In philosophical anthropology, self-transcendence refers
to all the ways in which human beings are drawn beyond external and internal
determinations into meaning, language, truth, subjectivity, creativity, self-
making and futurity.[6] As we have seen, self-transcendence in a formal (non-
ethical) sense has been depicted by Kierkegaard, Husserl, Heidegger,
Whitehead and many others. We note, however, that the human being can 'go
beyond' or transcend itself in all of these senses and at the same time be a
moral monster. The human being can be a passionate 'for itself' (Sartre) or a
future-oriented *Dasein* (Heidegger) and yet live the narcissistic existence of
the 'aesthetic stage', exist in the self-oriented world of a psychopathic
personality, or practise genocidal politics. In other words, the human being
can transcend itself formally as one who goes beyond that which would
prescribe and fix its being, or it can transcend itself ethically as one who feels
and acts from motivations other than self-survival and self-interest. Emmanuel
Levinas's primary contribution to philosophy was to press this distinction
between a merely formal self-transcendence and an ethical self-transcendence

in which the human being is seized and summoned to acknowledge the vulnerable, mortal, needy other. Contrasted to ethical transcendence, 'immanence' means indifference, apathy or obliviousness to the vulnerable other.

What do formal and ethical self-transcendence have to do with the *imago Dei*? They both constitute the very being of God. As freely and creatively active and not simply a passive mirror of external events, God is formally self-transcendent. As eternal Agape constantly seeking the good of what is other than Godself, God is ethically self-transcendent. Even if God is a self-transcending freedom (creativity) and a self-transcending love, how are such things connected to the *imago Dei*? First, if God is self-transcending freedom and self-transcending love, then to say that the human being is created in the divine image would mean that, in some way, it mirrors or embodies in finite form the divine freedom and the divine self-transcending compassion. Second, it is just these two self-transcendences that are presupposed by both human evil and redemptive remaking, because human evil, or sin, becomes a mere external causality if the human being is not a finite, self-transcending freedom, and it has no content to be distorted if it is not self-transcending love. Further, redemption takes on the character of a mere external determination if it does not engage a self-initiating freedom and, as a restoration, it would lack content and direction if the human being were not originally constituted as a self-transcending love. Accordingly, the human being resembles, or is the image of, God in both ways – as that which exists freely from itself, and as that which is summoned beyond itself toward the good of others.[7]

The divine image as formal self-transcendence (freedom) and ethical self-transcendence (compassionate responsibility) applies primarily to human individuals. Yet formal-self-transcendence presupposes a human inter-subjectivity that precedes and grounds individual freedom, futurity and creativity. Further, ethical self-transcendence spans both an individual phenomenon and a mutuality that arises between interresponsible others. The divine image is thus distributed over both individual and corporate modes of human experience.

The Image of God as Potentiality and Actuality

What exactly do we mean when we say that the human being is structurally constituted so as to be distortable by sin and redeemable by grace? What do sin and redemption presuppose as their conditions of possibility? A certain elusiveness pervades the old story of a pre-sin Eden – a story concerning what precedes human history. This elusiveness stands between us who live in history and the 'ideal' that sin and redemption presuppose. As Bonhoeffer says, we 'in the middle' – that is, in history – have only indirect and narrative access to what is original – that is, to the divine image as a presupposed structure.[8] In some views the divine image is simply a term for the human ideal. The Golden Age, utopia, original righteousness and eschaton all coalesce in that term. In these coalesced symbols of the ideal, the image of God and redemption have the same content. But, in another interpretation, the divine image describes a prehistorical, ambiguous mix of something actual (the human being's gift of certain divine traits) and something potential (the human being's intended destiny under God).[9] According to this latter view, sin arrested the potential aspect, the 'likeness' (*similitudo*), and exile from Eden (the entry into history) and ended or at least postponed the human being's fulfilled future. Whatever the outcome of the exegetical disputes concerning whether 'image' and 'likeness' are distinguishable, we face the theological question whether the idea of the divine image connotes both a sense of the human being as embodying a divine likeness and an unspecified potentiality realized only in redemption.

I have proposed that sin and redemptive transformation presuppose both self-transcending freedom and ethical self-transcending responsibility. A fuller account of self-transcending freedom would not only discuss formal freedom, temporality, subjectivity and language but also the elemental passions for self-existence, reality and intimate relations. Self-transcending freedom and its passions or desires perpetuate the human being's natural egocentrism.[10] The human being is naturally inclined towards satisfying its own biological, psychological and social needs. Ethical self-transcendence describes that which summons the human being out of its natural egocentric freedoms into the world and reality of the vulnerable other. Both formal and ethical self-transcendence constitute the divine image, not in the sense of redemption, but rather as an arrested mix of potentiality and actuality. In the symbolism of prehistory where potentiality and actuality are ambiguously mixed, egocentric formal and ethical self-transcendence exist as two antagonistic and exclusive moments or powers. In this situation, one or the other must rule, either the egocentric self-transcending passions or the summons of responsibility for the other. Hence, to be ethical means to suppress the passions. To be passionately subjective means to fail to heed the call of the vulnerable other. This tense relation of formal and ethical self-transcendence is the elusive, ambiguous potentiality of the structural presupposition of both sin and redemption.

The Imago Dei *as Beautiful*

When we enquire whether the presupposed divine image of the human being is beautiful, we face once again our historical legacy's competing interpretations of beauty. Even formal self-transcendence – that is, the human being constituted as transcendently temporal, as passionately subjective, or as an 'able-to-sin' free will (St Augustine) – does not lack a certain beauty. For to transcend or go beyond external or internal determination, to overcome the monotony of a fixed content, is to obtain self-differentiation over against mere unity. As formally self-transcendent, the human being differentiates itself from whatever constitutes its 'nature', 'essence' or content. The formal imago is, then, beautiful in the classical sense of unity in difference or, more aptly expressed, as an ongoing differentiating activity. According to this interpretation, the image of God is never sheer differentiation, but rather a creativity or freedom of something already constituted in a distinctive way.

But the human being is 'like God' not simply in its formal self-surpassing or freedom. For God is not simply a formal freedom but a compassionate consent (cf. Edwards) to the reality, goodness and need of what is other than God. It is this consent that constitutes God's eternal disposition to create and redeem. God's freedom, then, is never merely a formal freedom, a sheer possibility of action, but is the urge to share and procure good for what is other than God. And if we follow Jonathan Edwards, we will agree that this compassionate going-beyond, this ethical self-transcendence of consent, is the primordial instance and meaning of beauty. If sheer attractiveness is the criterion of the beautiful, we are surely more attracted to self-transcending love than we are to sheer proportion or harmony. Furthermore, if the human being is 'like God' not simply in its formal self-transcendence of being a subject but also as an ethical self-transcendence, able to be taken out of itself towards the needy other, its very constitution as a creature is marked by the primary beauty of consent to being. Both primary beauty (an ethical self-transcendence into the life of others) and formal self-transcending differentiation (self-creativity) describe the beauty of the *imago Dei*.[11]

Yet, this is only an individualized, and therefore abstract, account of the *imago Dei*. If an ethical self-transcendence characterizes the human being as the image of God, the human reality that both sin and redemption presuppose is not mere individuality, for ethical self-transcendence calls forth a human way of being together – an ethical mutuality. The human being as the image of God is an ethical mutuality forever correlated with formal and ethical self-transcendence. Thus the beauty of the *imago Dei* is distributed over both individual and interhuman modes of human reality. It is both the beauty of self-transcending consent to the needy other and the beauty of the mutual interrelation which arises therewith. Both of these beautiful modes of human reality are presupposed by the sin that distorts and weakens them and by redemption which carries them to a new level of actualization.[12]

The Despoiled Image

What does redemptive transformation reveal about its presupposed despoliation of human freedoms and desires by human evil?[13] We should be clear at this point that sin or human evil does not mean the natural competitiveness, aggressiveness and self-oriented satisfactions that attend all organic beings as they struggle to survive, mate and experience well-being. Only a world-denying asceticism and what has been labelled throughout Western Christian texts as 'Manichaeaism' would interpret organic, bodily life as intrinsically and essentially evil. In both Hebraic and Christian accounts, sin refers to another dimension of intention and action than simply organically-rooted behaviours. Most would agree that malice, murder, torture, coldheartedness and systemic oppression are evil. How do things of this sort originate? Arising in the shadowy mystery of human formal self-transcendence, sin does not lend itself to causal explanation. Yet the dynamics of human evil contain hints at something that activates evil. We human beings open ourselves to evil when, trying to secure ourselves against the scary, dangerous, unpredictable (chaotic) aspects of the world, we form absolute attachments to the attractive and powerful goods of the world. The evil things we do are almost always done in the name of these goods: religions, races, governments, tribes, heroes, causes, cult figures, territories, ideologies and world-views. In idolatrous mood, we expect these idols of the tribe to protect us against the very things that constitute our finitude: anxiety, boredom, ambiguity, uncertainty and tragedy. And with evil comes a different kind of self-orientation from the natural egocentrism associated with being a living organism. When self-orientation is shaped by an insistence on security, all things, even God, are measured by the degree to which they resolve the ambiguities and the deep anxieties of the finite self.

Both ancient and modern Christian theologies agree that these self-securing dynamics distort the divine image. But they have debated whether the image of God is simply distorted or completely obliterated. Those who contend for obliteration tend to think of the imago as a term for the Edenic, obedient and worshipful relationship with God. If that is the case, 'faith', expulsion from Eden, and original sin simply end that relationship and therefore the imago itself. In this view of the divine image, a totally destroyed imago would mean that human interrelation in history would utterly lack all mutual, ethical self-transcendence and mutual ethical orientations. Such a view that empties all peoples and all epochs of mutual ethical sensibilities is both empirically unconvincing and fatal to the structure which both human evil and redemptive transformation presuppose. On the other hand, if we think of the divine image as the ontological presupposition of human evil (that which undergoes distortion) and redemption (that which makes evil transformable), it becomes clearer how the imago is fractured by human evil.

I have contended that the image of God refers to both the formal conditions of human self-corruption (its formal self-transcendence as a subject) and ethical self-transcendence in which the human being is drawn beyond its natural egocentrism into an empathetic mutuality. Both of these anthropological conditions undergo distortion when evil creates a powerful dynamic of individual and interpersonal existence. The absolute attachments born of anxious self-securing transform the human being's benign natural egocentrism into the rapacious, manipulative and power-hungry creature that struts across the pages of human history. The human being's idolatrous agendas co-opt and transform formal self-transcendence, egocentrism and competitiveness. Ethical self-transcendence, by which the human being is drawn beyond its natural ego-centrism to exist on behalf of the vulnerable other, likewise sustains a blow. When evil sets the human agenda, the other is experienced as a potential threat to one's idols and is thus labelled in advance according to race, gender, ethnicity or nation. Ethical self-transcendence as a sensibility may not be totally destroyed in this reshaping, but it becomes subject to, and mixed with, relations of contempt, fear and management.

Conventional accounts of the way in which evil corrupts human beings tend to privilege moral discourse and the language of vices. Human beings, thus, are dishonest, selfish, cruel, insensitive and untrustworthy. It is rarely said that *evil* shapes the human being into something ugly. Insofar as beauty is thought to be proportion or harmony, there are grounds for saying that virtue harmonizes the conflicted self and is thus beautiful. If that is the case, to lack virtue is to be ugly.[14] But this Hellenic and medieval tradition of the beautiful, virtuous soul is an almost forgotten remnant in contemporary pieties and moral theologies. On the other hand, if Jonathan Edwards is our guide and we think of beauty as the ethical self-transcendence that consents to and loves what is other, there are strong grounds for thinking that sin performs an ugly work on human beings. The initial and most powerful work of sin is less the in-harmonious soul as the diminished ethically self-transcendent imago, a work that paralyses the self's capacity to relate empathetically to the other. In human history, this empathetic self-transcendence has not totally disappeared, but, shaped by sin, it tends to be restricted to the natural interrelations of family, friendship and one's ethnic or national group. When the imago falls under the power of idolatrous, anxious, self-securing, its capacity to transcend itself towards any and all others – natural, living, animal or human – is seriously curtailed. This curtailment cripples the aesthetic dimension of the human being and fosters two principal forms of ugliness: Philistinism and aestheticism.

Philistinism is the term for the fundamental effect of sin on the beautiful imago, a diminishment of the primary beauty of consenting, compassionate and empathetic self-transcendence.[15] To the degree that its ethical self-transcendence is diminished, the human being becomes ugly, and this effacement of the human being's primary beauty has serious secondary effects. Earlier chapters discussed the classical notion of beauty as harmony and the eighteenth-century's preoccupation with sensibility. Together, they describe the human being's enjoyment with, and sensibility to, beauty as being. The diminishment of ethical self-transcendence, the capacity to enter the world of the other, carries with it a lowered sensibility to the beauties of in-formed and processing being. This happens when natural egocentrism degenerates into fearful, idolatrous and self-securing ways of world engagement. The human being's need to manage, control, organize and fend off whatever threatens its idols replaces its engagement with what is consistently new, real and beautiful. The Philistine does not seek beauty but control and a managed life; the useful is the Philistine's primary concern. Wendell Berry, a Kentucky poet and essayist, eloquently urges resistance to Philistinism.

> Ask the questions that have no answers.
> Invest in the millennium. Plant sequoias.
> Say your main crop is the forest
>   that you did not plant;
> Say that the leaves are harvested
> When they have rooted into mold.
> Call that profit. Prophesy such returns.
> Put your faith in the two inches of humus
> That will build under the trees
> Every thousand years.[16]

The Philistine is too insistent on managing the world to take risks with what is really different, autonomously other or mysteriously beautiful. Hence, for the

Philistine, the beautiful means the pretty – something that can amuse, entertain, pay off.

Aestheticism is a second way by which the human being's relation to beauty becomes corrupted. Like any finite good, including even the ethical, beauty can become an idol. Even as laws, customs and 'values' can decline into moralism and legalism, so beauty can be taken captive by aestheticism: some pieties and theologies see any preoccupation with beauty as aestheticism. The term 'aestheticism' is not without its ambiguities.[17] It refers first of all to a mode of existence centered on aesthetic pleasure at the expense of the ethical, the religious or the cognitive. As previously stated, any finite good can vie for such a central position. Beauty is a powerful competitor for the centre precisely because of the intensity of the pleasure that it offers. A close examination yields an intriguing paradox at the very heart of aestheticism. To make beauty everything, to press beauty for its gifts, is to lose beauty. This loss can occur in two ways. First, aestheticism is a child of the distorted imago, and that means the abandonment of beauty as an ordinary and relative good for beauty as something able to be secured and found. A distorted egocentrism would use beauty to allay the anxieties that come with self-transcending temporality. The second way follows the path opened by the first. If beauty is there for one's use, if it is something to be 'experienced', then it must simply give pleasure. And to be oriented only to beauty's pleasure is to suppress the pathos that comes with the chaos, destabilization and the mystery of beauty. These elements are present both in the classical view of beauty as harmony and in the Edwardsian view of beauty as benevolence. To make 'pleasurable experience' beauty's point suppresses both forms of beauty and, like Philistinism, reduces beauty to the pretty.

Philistinism and aestheticism together diminish beauty in several different ways. Rooted in the distorted divine image with its diminished ethical self-transcendence, they reflect the ugliness of petty, mean, self-serving immanence. In addition, they effect a diminishment of sensibility to the beauty of the events, processes and entities of the world. The reshaping of the individual has been the focus of this analysis of the way sin distorts the beautiful imago. But because the human being is essentially and not accidentally intersubjective, formal and ethical self-transcendence also describe how human beings are bound together in consenting mutuality. Both the consenting heart and the consenting mutuality of human relations are beautiful. If that is the case, sin's corruption of the imago will carry with it a corruption of human interrelations: the diminishment of the individual's ethical self-transcendence will at the same time be an interhuman diminishment. Sin, in other words, threatens the aesthetic dimension of human interrelations, the beauty of consenting and benevolent mutuality. Accordingly, Philistinism and aestheticism are also phenomena of human interrelations and of actual, historical human societies and historical periods. Institutions, languages, world-views and deep values can embody and promote the Philistine uses of beauty and aestheticism's suppression of the pathetic side of beauty, thus reducing beauty to the pretty. In this way, Philistinism and aestheticism shape and endure in the institutions and even in whole epochs of human society.

Furthermore, throughout human history persist social systems so alienated from ethical self-transcendence that they target internal or external groups for systemic oppression. The targeted victims of such oppression are desensitized to beauty by slavery, meaningless labour, bureaucratic functions and structures of domestic, familial life. The poet, Edwin Markham, paints a grim picture of aesthetic loss brought about by systemic oppression. Speaking of a rural peasant removed from virtually all cultural privileges and consumed by dawn to dusk toil, he asks:

> Slave of the wheel of labor, what to him
> Are Plato and the swing of Pleiades?
> What the long reaches of the peaks of song,
> The rift of dawn, the reddening of the rose?[18]

And do these lines not also apply to postmoderns whose bureaucratic, professional and selling environments have little relation to the beautiful?

The Beauty of Redemptive Remaking

The subject of this inquiry is the place of beauty in the life of faith. 'The life of faith' is a telescoped expression for a redemptively transformed individual and community. The question, then, is not so much how beauty is part of an individual's or community's system of beliefs, for I have contended that faith, or redemptive existence, presupposes both the need of redemption (sin) and the possibility of redemption (the *imago Dei*). This would imply that the analysis should begin with redemptive remaking, not with its presupposed conditions. And it is the case that in the order of insight or understanding, it is the beauty of redemptive remaking that opens to us its presupposed conditions. On the other hand, it is of crucial importance to understand that beauty is always already part of the human scene, at work in its very creation and constitution. Accordingly, the analysis has begun with the primordial beauty of the imago fractured and diminished by evil. At this point we turn to beauty's most explicit self-manifestation, the redemptively transformed existence.

Redemptive Self-transcendence

The redemptive transformation of the human being is a multilayered affair that addresses the complex structure of formal self-transcendence, basic desires, various forms of world engagement, the interhuman and societal patterns. Presumably, redemption reaches and reshapes into new freedoms all the ways in which the human being is infected by sin. I shall bypass this formidable topic. Suffice it to say that the fundamental event that begins these remakings – the older theologies called it conversion, regeneration or justification – is a 'founding' in and by God that undermines the anxious need for idols and their security. The fundamental effect of this 'founding' is to draw the human being out of the self-preoccupied immanence that cripples its capacity to engage a genuine other. To use a metaphor from the text of Emmanuel Levinas, redemption awakens the human being from a kind of somnolence into an alert, open, empathetic, responsive and responsible insomnia.[19] In the corrupted imago, formal self-transcendence (being a subject, exercising imagination, existing temporally towards discerned future possibilities) becomes a field, even an instrument, of various idolatrous and destructive relations. One result of 'founding' and the reduction of the need for idols is that formal and ethical self-transcendence merge to overcome the exclusion between self-orientation and compassionate benevolence. Created in the divine image, the human being is 'like God' both as a formal self-transcendence and as one who empathetically transcends itself towards others. But in finite, historical form, natural egocentrism and generosity tend to compete with each other. The natural egocentrism of the survival-oriented organism conflicts with compassion and obligation. But the ideal or potential side of the divine image is an existence in which natural egocentrism, human subjectivity and basic desires are taken up into ethical self-transcendence. Redemptive self-transcendence is, then, the unity and harmonization of formal and ethical self-transcendence.

This 'founding' basic event of redemptive remaking carries with it a twofold beauty. First, being self-transcendently and compassionately disposed to the other and its need is an instance of what is most primordially beautiful. Second, the uniting of formal self-transcendence (and thus the various transcendings of the imagination, temporality, creativity and so on) with ethical self-transcendence is an instance of beauty as being – a proportion, harmony and unity in difference that shapes how the human being exists in the world.

Surmounting the Dichotomy of the Ethical and the Aesthetic

I have contended that redemption carries the beautiful but distorted imago to new levels of freedom. Such an interpretation counters and supplements those tendencies in Western moral thought which presuppose a dichotomy between the aesthetic and the ethical. Because such a dichotomy clearly undermines any notion of 'beautiful faith', it is important to overcome this apparently unbridgeable gap between beauty and responsibility.

Western texts which place beauty and the ethical in two unrelated domains (Whitehead is an exception) vary in their radicalism. We have seen that, in some texts, beauty is a feature of human transcendence (Kant) or of the transcending of everyday, routinized willing (Schopenhauer). Yet a trace of the dichotomy between beauty and the ethical lingers even in these formulations: in Kant by the placement of the ethical in the practical reason, distinguished from the imagination and pleasure-pain orientations; in Schopenhauer by his non-ethical account of the transcending of the will into representation (*Vorstellung*). Nevertheless, these texts do contain elements that soften the dichotomy. As differentiated moments in a sequential analysis, the cognitive, the practical and the aesthetic of Kant seem to be separate human faculties; on the other hand, as dimensions of human world engagement, they are closely intertwined and interdependent. And it is fair to say that for Kant, both cognitive (pure) and ethical (practical) reason presuppose the more primordial, pleasure–pain orientation where beauty resides. For Schopenhauer the transcending of the enslaving subject–object orientation of the will by way of the beautiful is a kind of redemption that resembles an ethic.

In the philosophical programme of Emmanuel Levinas, the dichotomy of the aesthetic and the ethical is radicalized. We must acknowledge that this is not a metaphysical dichotomy, an ontological partitioning of the human being. In the Levinas texts the ethical has no ontological status precisely because it is what confronts, restrains and issues a summons to every sense in which the human being is being. Thus, for Levinas, all the transcendences that we find in Kant, Kierkegaard, Schopenhauer, Husserl and others – the transcendences of passionate subjectivity and the beauty-engaged imagination – remain in the realm of immanence. There is nothing in Levinas's philosophy that would require him to withhold beauty from these transcendences, but he must with-hold it from the ethical. Like Karl Barth, Levinas is not a correlationist. The ethical as a display of the infinite in the vulnerable face of the other simply lays hold of, summons and dominates. It does not negotiate, engage motives or appeal to points of contact.

We must then ask ourselves whether this tradition of dichotomy present, in a qualified fashion, in Kant and Schopenhauer and radicalized in Levinas forestalls a theological aesthetic that discovers beauty primordially in the *imago Dei* and claims that ethical self-transcendence itself is beautiful. At this point we pose to the Levinas text the following question. How is it that a vulnerable alterity can evoke a summons into *responsibility*? Levinas's notion of how the human face draws the other into empathetic responsibility is not a metaphor of external causality. Even though the face 'seizes', dominates and summons, *what* it seizes is not a mere thing, an inert substance. How is it that the face's summons can be heeded? Certain kinds of entities (stones, chemicals and planets) do not heed it. The ethical does not arise with these things. Because the ethical takes place in a human order, it presupposes that something about the human being is not able to be indifferent or completely oblivious to the victimizable face of the other. Why does not a vulnerable, victimizable alterity (face) evoke simply indifference? Why could not the human being respond to the vulnerable other with mere contempt, ridicule or callous hardheadedness? Levinas would agree that the human being can be summoned, seized by the vulnerable other only if it senses the pathos in that vulnerability. But what renders the vulnerable other pathetic? Why does suffering engage, appeal to, awaken or summon one into obligation?

I submit that something is at work in the summons of the face that gives it a power to evoke responsibility – namely, the other's fragile beauty. However, this beautiful alterity present in the vulnerable other is not simply the secondary beauty of proportion. It is not simply the other's harmonious (integrated) self or bodily grace that renders it pathetically beautiful. All actual finite entities combine elements of chaos (fragility) and harmony. But the human other presents a different sort of fragile beauty. We recall that, for Edwards (and theology), primary beauty is the self-transcending disposition of the heart to consent to, acknowledge and seek the good of the other. Is the other reducible to mere fragility? Is that which evokes consent a contentless and abstract neediness? Both theological and philosophical considerations prompt a negative answer. Theologically speaking, the other as the divine image is always already constituted as formally and ethically self-transcending. To meet an other is thus not to meet a nothing, a chaos, a mere object or an essence, nor is it to meet something whose only message is one of threat and competition. However diminished and distorted by historical evil, the imago disposes the other to empathetically transcend itself.

Philosophically speaking, to engage an other is to experience a kind of acknowledgement. One senses that the other is not simply obliviously or ignorantly grasping one's self as a mere thing. This is why Sartre's account of human intersubjectivity is so limited and impoverished. In Sartre's view the look (*le regard*) of the other is simply an objectifying, annihilation of one's self-transcending subjectivity (or being for-itself).[20] Sartre is right to say that the other, as other, cannot coincide with our own subjectivity and immanence; as other, it is always an external perspective on our subjectivity. Yet this external perspective is not reducible to, or exhausted by, an act of objectification. One does not experience in the look of the other an utter refusal of one's subjectivity, a mere reduction to thingness, but rather a self-transcending acknowledgement of one's own non-reducibility. Even attitudes and acts of malice, cruelty, manipulation and stereotyping, even sexist, racist, and ethnic attempts to reduce to labels, are all built on this acknowledgement. The other knows at some primordial level that I am a non-reducible self-transcendence. Thus, the other is a vulnerable, murderable face, but what makes it murderable is the fragile beauty of its self-surpassing consent, its acknowledgement of a subjectivity not its own. Accordingly, we are engaged by the vulnerability of the other because the beauty of its self-transcendence renders it pathetic. In other words, an interhuman relation of mutual consent and acknowledgement (the *imago Dei*) is at work in the summons of the vulnerable face that draws the human being out of itself into responsibility. In short, a self-transcending consent is what evokes a sense of the other's fragility. This is why beauty (the aesthetic) is not simply outside the ethical as some other capacity or dimension of the human being. Rather, beauty is present already in the ethical in three quite different ways. First, the ethical presupposes the beauty of formal self-transcendence, the harmonies or proportions that come with all experience and with all world engagements. Second, the beauty of the other as a consenting being is part of the vulnerability that draws the human being into the ethical. Third, ethical self-transcendence is the primary instance of what is beautiful.

Faith's Aesthetic Sensibilities

The chapter so far has pressed a single thesis, that beauty comes with redemptive transformation and its presupposed structure of *imago Dei* and sin, that the consenting, benevolent self and of its reciprocal relations are beautiful. But redemptive remaking invariably sets up tremors throughout the various dispositions, feelings, relations and activities of the human being. It is at this point that the eighteenth-century motif of aesthetic sensibility comes to our assistance. It is also just at this point that certain kinds of theology become suspiciously anti-aesthetic. The Gospel, so they might say, is about Jesus, the incarnation, justification and a heavenly destiny. Thus, to add aesthetic sensibility to these themes and, with that, nature, process and world, allows natural theology to rear its ugly head. I can only suspect that such a response is covertly, or not so convertly, dominated by a forensic type of thinking that identifies redemption with a divinely effected status change, and is thus unable to recognize how redemption actually transforms the whole *eros* or desire structure of the human being. If redemption does in fact transmute corrupted human desires into new freedoms, it must bring about what Edwards called 'dispositions' – tendencies to feel, think and act in certain directions and not in others. Surely only a solipsistic and Cartesian mindset would limit redemptive transformation to the 'interior' self, thus denying its effects on ways in which human beings relate to both human others and all of creation? Conventional pieties express such redemption in largely moral terms: altruistic actions, conformity to sexual mores, familial obligations and moderation of the appetites. Here, too, a presupposed dichotomy between beauty and the ethical is at work, played out as a refusal to allow aesthetic sensibility and world engagement into the life of faith and piety.

How is it that the aesthetic dimension of redemptive existence gives rise to a sensibility to the beautiful? More specifically, how does the beauty of the restored imago and of ethical self-transcendence engender orientations, dispositions and sensibilities to what is beautiful? I have tried to show that a discernment of the beauty of the other's self-surpassing consent is at work in ethical self-transcendence. We recall at this point that ethical self-transcendence means going beyond mere residence inside one's self-oriented needs and desires in dispositions of care and consent for the other. As Edwards argues, this consent is 'true virtue' only if it has no qualifications and no selected, privileged objects. In other words, it is 'consent to being'. Ethical self-transcendence is this orientation to being, to any and all genuine others in their distinctive reality, complexity, mystery and even danger. Further, it should be evident that one cannot be consentingly oriented to the other and at the same time be indifferent or obtuse to its beauty. It would seem that the initial sphere of this orientation of consent and benevolence is the human world, but with this self-transcending benevolence towards the human other comes a certain momentum, an expanding teleology that opens itself to the beauty of any and all others. Sensibility to the beauty of the human other's acknowledgement at work in the divine image and restored in redemption becomes sensibility to any and all beauty.

It is at this point that we recall the Hellenic–medieval tradition of beauty as being. If redemptive self-transcendence opens the human being to the mysterious, elusive, fathomless reality of all finite others, to 'all this juice and all this joy', as Hopkins says,[21] it is at the same time open to what has pushed it out of chaos, the patterns, shapes, colours and lingering smells of the world, the ever re-forming, processing newness of the 'creative advance'.[22] Such an aesthetic orientation is spontaneous and immediate to piety and faith. It is not spawned as the conclusion of a sequence of reasoning that argues that, because God made the world, one 'should' appreciate it. As the divine image, the human being is already constituted as formally and ethically self-transcending and thus oriented, at least in its recondite identity, beyond itself to others. Redemptive transformation restores, intensifies and carries to new levels this orientation. It can be argued (cf. Whitehead) that every living thing is oriented to beauty insofar as any and all perception, however primitive, is qualitatively a kind of satisfaction. For to be perceived at all, an entity must have minimum form, continuity and differentiation within its environment. Redemptive self-transcendence prompts world engagements marked by an intensified sense of the beauty of being, of the 'dearest freshness deep down things'.[23] Once the human being is released back into benevolence, generosity and consent (ethical self-transcendence), it cannot but have an intensified sensibility to what the *Religio Medici* calls 'the general beauty of the works of God'. The American poet, Edward Arlington Robinson, catches the mood when he has Lancelot say, '. . . I've always liked this world, and I would a deal rather live in it than leave it in the middle of all this music'.[24]

But beauty as being is not simply the geometric, proportional aspect of entities but also the unpredictable newness of the flow of things. It also means the inevitable grace of a living body as it movingly negotiates the world of space, place, time and gravity. We need not think of bodily grace as the sole possession of dancers and great athletes, and thus diminished in the rest of us or absent in the disabled. We display bodily grace in the simple movements of hands, in walking, in facial expressions, and in bodily postures that are not just stiff, fearful, or haughty. And unless we embrace an absolute body and self dualism, we must acknowledge that the sensibilities to beauty that originate with redemptive self-transcendence carry over into bodily comportment. In other words, the aesthetic sensibilities that attend redemptive remaking include orientation to the differentiated pattern of being, to the flow of processing differentiation and bodily grace. These sensibilities may, of course, take the form of orientations to art or even find artistic expression. But the arts cannot define or exhaust the sensibilities that arise when the Philistinisms and aesthetisms of the despoiled imago are transformed by redemption.

Notes

1   Jonathan Edwards, *Freedom of the Will*, ed. Paul Ramsey (New Haven, CT: Yale University Press, 1957), p. 166.

2   Armand Maurer, *About Beauty: A Thomist Interpretation* (Houston: University of St Thomas, 1983), p. 65.

3   C.S. Lewis, *Till We Have Faces: A Myth Re-told* (San Diego: Harcourt, Brace and Co., 1939), pp. 80–81.

4   On the *imago Dei* as a theological and not just exegetical inquiry, see Emil Brunner, *Man in Revolt*, trans. Olive Wyon (Philadelphia: Westminster Press, 1947), p. 503.

5   David Cairns expresses the point as follows. 'Thus, when Christ saves us, he saves what has always been his, though it had fallen from him': *The Image of God in Man* (London: SCM, 1953). The divine image, then, is 'an inescapable relation of responsibility to God and man' (p. 196). Similarly, Emil Brunner rejects Calvin's term of 'relic' to describe the imago (although he himself goes on to speak of 'traces' of the image in the human structure, in addition he eschews the expression of a 'formal image' since this calls up the ancient

notion of double image (imago and *similitudo*). Yet, he would speak of the *humanitas* in its 'formal character' as 'that which man has retained of his original relation to God, and the power of creating order in human life, and point of contact': *Man in Revolt*, p. 514.

6 These concepts express various post-Cartesian departures from the classical Platonic and Aristotelian philosophical anthropologies. All the departures understand the human being to be a self-transcending, existential temporality. This is not to say, however, that pre-Cartesian Western philosophy had no sense of human self-transcendence. In Plato and Aristotle, what enables the human to surpass external and internal determination is reason (*logos, nous, epistemé*). To have the power to grasp world arrangements – cosmic and political – is not to be simply fated to and enslaved by institutional, personal, or mythological causalities. And it was this way of understanding self-transcendence as the intelligence-empowered soul that dominated theology from Irenaeus through the Middle Ages. Typical of the patristic period was Origen's contention that the imago does not refer to human physical appearance ('formed' from the primordial slime) but to the 'inner human being' which is incorporeal and incorruptible – traits of divine being itself: *Genesis*, Homily I.

7 Two quite different ways of interpreting the image of God are common in the history of Christian theology. In the one (formal), the imago consists in such human powers as reason or freedom of choice, or whatever enables the human being to rule over animal creation. In the other (ethical), the imago is the human being's holiness or moral perfections. Both versions occur in the patristic period. For Origen, the imago was the 'reasonable soul': *Against Celsus*, Chapter 63, origin *Contra Celsum*, trans. Henry Chadwick (New York/Cambridge: Cambridge University Press, 1980). A similar view is held by Athanasius, *Contra gentiles and De Incarnatione*, trans. R.W. Thompson (Oxford: Clarendon Press, 1971). ('Against the Gentiles', #34) and St Augustine, *City of God against the Pagans*, Chapter 23, trans. R.W. Dyson (Cambridge/New York: Cambridge University Press, 1998). For Chrysostom, the imago meant the human being's superior, governing position over all creatures by way of reason and intelligence. Gregory of Nyssa held to the ethical imago; thus the human being resembled God in its 'purity', wisdom, virtue, freedom from passion and alienation from all evil. And Irenaeus, *St Iranaeus of Lyon against the Heresies*, trans. D.J. Unger (New York: Paulist Press, 1992), who may be the primary instigator of the doctrine of the divine image articulated both a formal (imago) and ethical (*similitudo*) resemblance (*Against Heresies*, Chapter 16). The Reformed Scholastic theologies of the seventeenth century distinguished between the *imago Dei intrinseca* (the faculties of intellect, will, and conscience) and the *imago Dei extrinseca* (the faculties of righteousness, holiness and purity). See Richard A. Muller, *Dictionary of Latin and Greek Theological Terms Drawn Principally from Protestant Scholastic Theology* (Grand Rapids, MI: Baker Book House, 1985), p. 145.

8 Dietrich Bonhoeffer, *Creation and Fall*, trans. J.C. Fletcher (London: SCM Press, 1959), pp. 12–13.

9 Early patristic theology (Irenaeus) made this distinction between the original innocence of Edenic human being and its intended but lost fulfilment. Paul Tillich demythologizes the Irenaean notion of an actual pre-Fallen state of innocence by reincorporating the notion as an ever-present 'dreaming innocence' of human history and experience: *Systematic Theology*, Vol. II (Chicago: University of Chicago Press), p. 33.

10 For a detailed treatment of the place of natural egocentrism in a theological anthropology and its relation to sin and to human remaking, see the author's *Good and Evil: Interpreting a Human Condition* (Minneapolis: Augsburg Fortress, 1990), pp. 181–82, 190–91, 244–47.

11 Early and medieval Christian theology almost never described the divine image as beautiful. Gregory of Nyssa is an exception. As King God has a royal dignity, thus to be created in God's image is to resemble something royal. However, what specifically constitutes the resemblance is not the paraphernalia of the royal (purpose colours, scepter) but kingly virtue, 'the most royal of all raiment'. Reflecting God's virtue, the human being 'is shown to be perfectly like to the beauty of its archetype in all that belongs to the dignity of Royalty': 'On the Making of Man', in *Nicene and PostNicene Fathers*, Second Series, Vol. V (New York: Christian Literature Co., 1893), #IV.

12   In most Christian theologies, the *imago Dei*, especially as a formal expression of distinctive human powers, functions to set the human being apart from the 'brutes' and the rest of nature. Human beings, therefore, possess reason and freedom of the will: creatures (except angels) do not. I would prefer to think that all creatures embody varying ways of being self-transcendent and therefore both sides of the divine image. That is, no creature is utterly reducible to passivity, to external and internal causalities, and no creature is utterly reducible to solipsistic self-concern and indifference toward the others of its life-world.

13   For an extensive treatment of how human evil corrupts and weakens human desires, see Farley, *Good and Evil*, Chapters 9–11.

14   Texts on the ugliness of sin or human evil are rare in Christian theology. We are more likely to find such texts in sermons, poetry, and works on spirituality. William Langland's fourteenth-century *Piers Plowman* is an example. In this work Langland personifies the seven deadly sins. Thus, *covetousness* is described as a figure who had 'beetling brows and thick, puffy lips, and his eyes were as bleary as a blind old hag's. His baggy cheeks sagged down below his chin, flapping about like a leather wallet, and trembling with old age. His beard was all bespattered with grease. He wore a hood on his head with a lousy cap on top, and a dirty-brown smock at least a dozen years old, torn and filthy and crawling with lice': *Piers Plowman*, trans. J.F. Goodridge (Harmondsworth: Penguin Books, 1959), p. 105. The other deadly sins are similarly portrayed as gross, disgusting and ugly. This tradition of the ugliness (loathsomeness) of the deadly sins continues in the sixteenth century in Edmund Spenser's *The Faerie Queene*. Accordingly, the temptress, Lucifera, a self-appointed queen, seemingly beautiful, is decked out in glittering adornments. But the beasts that draw her chariot, her hidden energies, are the deadly sins: gluttony as a 'filthy swine', avarice like a 'vile disease'. Spenser employs the language of disgust, frightfulness and death to describe these sins. See Book One, Canto IV, pp. 12–36.

15   For a contemporary interpretation of Philistinism, see Frank Burch Brown, *Religious Aesthetics: A Theological Study of Making and Meaning* (Princeton, NJ: Princeton University Press, 1989), p. 153.

16   Wendell Berry, 'Manifesto: the Mad Farmer's Liberation Front', *Collected Poems: 1957–1982* (Berkeley, CA: North Point Press, 1985), p. 151.

17   Among the variety of meanings of the term 'aestheticism', are the following: the placing of aesthetic values above all other values (expressed, for instance, in many of the witticisms of Oscar Wilde), the self-understanding of the artistic community at the end of the nineteenth century, expressed in the phrase, 'art for art's sake' (cf. Victor Cousin), an art- or beauty-based world-view contrasted to their ethical or theological perspectives. For an analysis of aestheticism and its many meanings, see A. Halder, 'Aesthetizismus', in Joachim Ritter (ed.), *Historiche Wörterbuch de Philosophie*, Vol. 1 (Basel/Stuttgart: Schwebed Co.). Frank Burch Brown identifies two forms of aestheticism: an 'idolatry of aesthetic experience *per se*' and 'the theoretical assimilation of the religious and the moral to the aesthetic on the assumption that art and beauty are intrinsically redemptive': *Religious Aesthetics*, p. 152.

18   Edwin Markham, 'The Man with the Hoe', in Roy J. Cook (ed.), *One Hundred and One Famous Poems* (Chicago: The Cable Co., 1929), p. 55.

19   Emmanual Levinas, 'God and Philosophy', in *Collected Philosophical Papers*, trans. A. Lingis (The Hague: Nijhoff, 1987), pp. 155–56.

20   Jean-Paul Sartre, *Being and Nothingness*, Part III, trans. Hazel Barnes (New York: Philosophical Library, 1956), Chapter One, (IV).

21   Gerard Manley Hopkins, 'Spring', *The Poems of Gerard Manley Hopkins*, 2nd edition (London/New York/Toronto: Oxford University Press, 1938), p. 27.

22. 'On the contrary, the experience of the beautiful and particularly the beautiful in art, is the invocation of a potentially whole and holy order of things, wherever it may be found.' Hans Georg Gadamer, 'The Relevance of the Beautiful', in *The Relevance of the Beautiful and Other Essays*, trans. N. Walker (Cambridge: Cambridge University Press, 1986), p. 32.

23   Gerard Manley Hopkins, 'God's Grandeur', *Poems of Gerard Manley Hopkins* (London: Oxford University Press, 1930), p. 26.

24   Edward Arlington Robinson, 'Lancelot', *Collected Poems* (New York: The Macmillan Co., 1937), p. 432.

Chapter 8

Beauty, Pathos and Joy

The loveliest thing earth hath, a shadow hath,
A dark and livelong hint of death,
Haunting it ever till its last faint breath . . . (Walter de la Mare)[1]

. . . a loveliness so gay
that joy was in the eyes of every saint. (Dante)[2]

Yea, of this complex I believe mine eyes
Behind the universal form – in me,
Even as I speak, I feel such joy arise. (Dante)[3]

Earlier chapters of this book narrated not only the Western tale of beauty but also beauty's Cinderella status in Western Christian piety and theology. They also reviewed several conceptual polarities or dichotomies that contribute to, and confirm, piety's suspicion of beauty: for instance, beauty and the ethical, beauty and faith, the aesthetic and the practical. Two dichotomies that work to suppress beauty remain to be treated. According to the one, beauty (and aesthetics) falls on the trivial, shallow side of human experience because, having to do with what satisfies and fulfils, it must suppress all pathos and pain. According to the other, beauty falls on the hedonistic or pleasureable side of human experience, and hence inevitably corrupts the rigorous, discipline-oriented tasks of ethical and practical life. It remains now to explore these two dichotomies, and then to bring the book to a conclusion by portraying how grim is the life of faith without beauty.

Beauty and Pathos

The previous chapter yielded two conclusions: that the redemptively transformed imago is itself beautiful, and that redemption engenders sensibilities to beauty in all of its forms. To some, aesthetic sensibility is simply an orientation to what bestows an intrinsic and not just useful pleasure or satisfaction. Beauty, thus, will have no intercourse with pain, shadow, or frustration, the very things that give depth and mystery to life. A full and genuine sensibility to beauty can only be paradoxical, open both to what attracts and what saddens. How can beauty invite what appears to be its opposite into its chambers? Our initial intuition is that, because beauty pleases and ugliness saddens, they cannot be combined. According to the 'great theory of beauty' as proportion, beauty comes with being because nothing can 'be' without some differentiation, some continuity over time, some distinctive content that unifies the entity. Both

101

mythologies (Hesiod) and philosophies (Plato, Whitehead) of beauty agree
that pattern, form, unity and 'satisfying' concrescence all come about against,
and in relation to, what is not simply pattern or form – namely chaos, a term
which covers the indeterminate, the destructive, the trivial and even the mono-
tonous. However, chaos is never simply something in the past which in-formed
or concrescing entities have left behind. It persists into, and is contemporary
with, all entities. If chaos were utterly in the past, no entity could change from
one state to another. If possibility, accident and self-initiation had no part in
the present, creativity and the flow of things would cease. Chaos, then, is a
general term for all those elements without which nothing can come about, or
obtain differentiation, pattern, or continuity: elements of chance, possibility,
time, freedom, incompatibility of aim and competitiveness.[4] Without these
things, nothing would 'be'. And without these things, nothing would be perceived as beautiful. To experience beauty as harmony, unity in difference, or
as fitting, is to simultaneously comprehend accident, confusion and the spaces
and times that make change possible. In other words, it is to simultaneously
grasp chaos. One cannot experience one's own graceful body in motion without
also understanding the elements against and through which it makes its efforts
– the ever-present possibility of failed bodily acts in the face of gravity,
weakness, miscalculated spaces and accidental environmental events. These
persisting, ever-present elements of chaos is beauty's pathos.[5] And to experience
or participate in beauty is to apprehend not only the fitting and the harmonious
but also the accidental and the perilous.

At the same time, we recall Edwards' contention that harmony (or proportion)
is not what is primarily beautiful. Primary beauty is a disposition and act of
benevolent consent, primordially present as God's self-transcending generosity
and dependently displayed in the loveliness of human virtue. But since
benevolence is a response to need, lack, absence and what is non-ideal, there
is no benevolence without pathos. To be benevolently disposed is caringly to
move beyond natural egocentrism into the world of the vulnerable, needy
other. Benevolence, then, is a relation, a way of being engaged with the other,
and a certain discernment or sensibility always accompanies this relation. To
lack this sensibility is to be indifferent, obtuse and callous toward the other.

In the preceding modification (Chapter 7) of Levinas's interpretation of
ethical self-transcendence, I contended that the other's fragile beauty played a
part in the seizing power of its vulnerability. All finite beings combine proportion and chaos, beauty (harmony) and pathos (accident, the non-ideal and
mortality). But a deeper pathos tracks historical human beings. First, their
mortality is not simply a cold, objective quality like the eventual erosion of a
mountain, but rather a feature of their formal self-transcendence. As a linguistic,
meaning-ridden, imaginative, and future-oriented entity – in other words, as
passionate subjectivity – the human being is intensely self-aware of the time
limitation built into its existence. Thus, the chaos or tragic element of all finite
things is reinscribed on the human being as a pathetic self-consciousness.
Human pathos is the world's pathos become self-aware.

To discerningly enter the life of a human other is to participate not only in
its beauty but its pathetic self-consciousness. But a more radical pathos than

self-aware mortality besets the historical human being. Its individual and social existence is fractured by the effects of human evil. The dynamics of idolatry alters biologically-rooted natural competitiveness into malicious, genocidal, oppressive social systems. Hence, to discern and care for the fragile beauty and fractured existence of a human other is a kind of suffering. This suffering is not accidental – that is, something that arises only when the other disappoints or fails. Intrinsic to historical human intersubjectivity, suffering necessarily attends human sensibility to the finite, self-transcending pathos and fractured being of the other.

Beauty, then, is paradoxical because chaos and pathos always lurk at the edges of harmony and benevolence. Thus, we can see why the human being, intent on ridding itself of all anxiety and negativity, would suppress beauty by way of ascetic denial or reduction to the pretty. The idols of historical evil exact a dreadful toll when their promise of absolute security is taken seriously. Anxiously self-preoccupied and attached to all sorts of self-securing loyalties and obsessions, the human being flees from the world's chaos element. Driven by idols, the human being has little tolerance for the tragic, the uncertain, the surprises of the future, the pathos of nature and life, and the deeper pathos of human reality. And to deny pathos is to deny reality. Further, to refuse beauty's pathos is to trivialize beauty and reduce it to the safe, the tame, the pretty and the repetitive. In G.K. Chesterton's words, 'There is one sin, to call a green leaf gray.'[6] Accordingly, beauty fares better in religions and cultures that find a way of accepting and symbolizing the world's tragic aspect. It fares worse when religions include in their narratives and rituals only the ideal dimension: that is, the triumphant future, the exactly arranged justice and the geometrically perfect cosmos.

It should now be clear why redemptive transformation brings about a deepened sensibility to beauty. Blocking that sensibility is the self-securing and anxious suppression of the chaos of the world and the pathos of the human story. If redemption so 'founds' the human being that it is free to consent to a perilous and contingent finitude, it can replace the 'denial of death'[7] with a courageous consent to the paradoxical mix of chaos and order, beauty and pathos. Without that consent and orientation, the human being insists on a safe, tame, and predictable world and, in so doing, becomes obtuse to scary beauty. In the words of the American poet, Vassar Miller:

> May I not be like those who spit out life
> Because they loathe the taste, the smell, the muss
> Of happiness mixed with the herb of grief.[8]

Joy: Beyond the Dichotomy of Rigorism and Satisfaction

A second dichotomy that would block beauty's entrance into the world of faith is the apparent rift between faith's rigorism (self-discipline, obedience, justice, law and responsibility) and pleasure or emotional satisfaction.[9] To expose the flawed character of this dichotomy calls for an exploration of that which carries the apparent either-or to another plane – namely joy.

According to some interpretations, redemptive self-transcendence means simply moral self-transcendence, an abandonment of all self-concerns for the sake of the other. In this view positive pleasures are suspect. There seems to be no place for pleasure, happiness, or emotional satisfaction in the life of faith. Pleasure comes only with eschatological fulfilment, a reward for the self-denying ascetic, the martyr or the saint. Pleasure is a legitimate 'then' but an illegitimate 'now'. And if sensibility to beauty brings pleasure, then to postpone pleasure is also to postpone beauty. Conversely, to acknowledge beauty's place in the life of faith is to grant to faith a hedonistic aspect. This affirmation of pleasure or satisfaction is the final step of this theological aesthetic.

To discover in the very heart of faith a hedonistic element is surely a risky business. Popular religion throughout the world seems to have a powerful hedonistic element that engages human self-interests. Religion helps human beings survive devastating 'acts of God', be happy, have peace of mind, and live forever in some heavenly place. This trait of popular religion is enormously exacerbated in what Christopher Lasch calls the modern culture of narcissism.[10] In the last 50 years, many of the magazines, gurus, television programmes and religious movements of North American popular religion have made hedonism Christianity's central focus. Career success, physical health and inner peace are offered as rewards for faith. Reacting against the prevailing narcissistic tone of postmodern culture and 'happiness religion', some of us are ready to dissociate faith from happiness, pleasure and satisfaction. Accordingly, I shall promote faith's hedonistic dimension in the face of two dubious traditions: the one (asceticism) that would exclude pleasure from the realm of faith, the other (narcissistic religion) that would make it all in all. Two motifs may help us see how a sensibility to beauty both expresses and limits the hedonistic element in faith, the relation between beauty and pathos and joy.

I have maintained that to experience beauty is also to experience pathos. Does such a thesis neutralize itself? Does the admission of pathos into the halls of beauty undermine the aesthetic by turning it into a paralysing struggle between opposing forces of harmony and chaos, appreciation and suffering? Does beauty wither on the vine of ambiguity? This would be the case if paradox were the last word in setting the relationship between pathos and beauty. We must therefore determine whether pathos and beauty are mere competitors, mere equal partners in faith's sensibility to beauty.

I begin by observing that certain kinds of entities and occasions do evoke responses that are primarily fearful, angry or painful. In such instances the negative is the dominating tone. Furthermore, certain bittersweet experiences mix satisfaction and sadness: as William Shakespeare's Juliet says, 'Parting is such sweet sorrow'. But the experience of beauty is neither primarily negative nor merely ambiguous. Meaning, perception, insight and emotion all figure into the sensibility to beauty. But we fail to do justice to that sensibility when we think of it as a self-neutralizing, ambiguous confrontation between negation and affirmation. To sense the beauty of another's compassion, the abstract beauty of a geometrical design or the 'brute beauty' of the 'daylight's dauphin, and apple-dawn-drawn Falcon, in his riding' is not to be paralysed by hesitation or conflicted emotions.[11] Chaos may be an element in all these things, even in the geometrical form, but it is not what so dominates the sensibility as to be that which seizes, evokes and takes one out of oneself. As to the harmoniously united entity, it is the proportion itself that powerfully draws the human being into self-transcendence. As to the human other, it is the astonishing beauty of the consenting, benevolent disposition that overrides cynicism, indifference and doubt.

Accordingly, pathos is an ever-present and intrinsic element in beauty but always as derivative and marginal, something that lurks in every passage of time as a presupposed indeterminacy and perilous possibility. To be sure, it is always possible to redirect one's attention to what is marginal and derivative, to become preoccupied with beauty's pathetic aspect, and thus thematize non-being, anxiety, disturbance, peril and the like. But to do that is to break the spell of beauty. What dominates the sensibility to beauty is not what is marginal but what attracts, satisfies and gives pleasure. This is even the case in those instances of beauty in which awesomeness, danger and mystery are intense to the point of being overwhelming – namely the sublime. Even the sublime entity with its hints of infinity and awesome mystery is not a mere combination of harmony and chaos. Yet we must be careful not to say that only what is sublimely beautiful possesses mystery, infinity and chaos. These elements haunt every beautiful thing. The sublime describes a beautiful object in which the chaos, infinity (vastness) and mystery are greatly increased. Even so, the increase does not overwhelm the proportioned entity or the loving disposition so as to render it marginal or merely ambiguous.

Our second motif, joy, directly confronts Christian rigorism. Rigorism or asceticism need not be pejorative terms. Their defining dynamic need not be the suppression of pleasure but rather the importance of personal and communal discipline in service of moral ends and compassionate activities. Prophets, revolutionaries, 'doctors of the Church', feminists and contemplatives are all rigorists of a sort. But Christian history has seen a type of asceticism built on the assumption that the necessary condition for the highest level of spirituality is the suppression of human pleasure – bodily, sexual, perceptual, entertaining, playful. Extreme forms of this suppression punish the body with pain and misery. In addition, a comfort-denying rigorism has shaped the piety and discourse of certain eras of the Protestant movement. This deep suspicion of pleasure has roots both in pre-Christian asceticism and in the failure of churchly pieties to evoke positive theologies of happiness and pleasure. Behind the failure is the assumption that orientation to pleasure is the child of a corrupted immanence and idolatrous egocentrism. This assumption fails to grasp the way in which redemption transforms idolatrous desires and releases them into new freedoms. And this poses our question. If faith and redemptive trans-formation do evoke self-transcending responsibility, how can they at the same time engender self-satisfaction, pleasure and happiness?

Even in its most powerful and intense forms, pathos never entirely displaces the pleasure or satisfaction evoked by harmony or benevolence. Pleasure in the world's harmonies appears to be universal in human history and is probably an aspect of experience in all forms of life. But the pleasures that come with the world's flow into form should not be confused with the positive satisfaction always to be found in the life of faith. At this point it is important to differentiate pleasure and joy. Eating tasty cuisine, having a massage and solving a puzzle are pleasures. Similarly, religious fantasies about life in heaven marked by sounds of harps and freedom from the pains and anxieties of organic life are mostly about pleasures. We may sometimes speak of these things as enjoyments: we rarely think of them as providing joy. Joy arises only when there is a transcending of egocentric pleasure into the life of the other. Joy, in other words, is a phenomenon of ethical self-transcendence. A unique 'pleasurable' quality or tone of experience marks ethical self-transcendence. Drawn to the strange, self-transcending beauty of the other and oriented to its need and welfare, the human being experiences joy. Joy, then, is the experiential quality of the orientation of ethical self-transcendence. Its primary dynamic is not 'something I need has been given to me'. It is, rather, 'this beautiful, vulnerable other is coming to be as itself'. It is therefore a state of participation in the 'world' of the other, a residing mood (not just a passing emotion) that comes with empathetic caring. Here, too, the primordial instance of joy is God's loving and creative participation in what is other than itself.

It should be clear that the primary tone of redemptive transformation as ethical self-transcendence is joy.[12] This does not mean the pleasant and positive 'feelings' that accompany conversion, worship or contemplation. Such events of human psychological and communal life are authentically part of the world of faith only as signs of redemptive transformation. Drawn into empathetic life with the other, the human being then praises God, experiences the divine presence and contemplates divine mysteries. Apart from ethical self-transcendence, worship and praise remain instances of natural egocentrism and even idolatrous self-securing.

If redemption brings about ethical self-transcendence and empathetic participation in the world of the other, then a deep pleasure in the form of joy characterizes the life of faith. If faith (redemption) were simply for the sake of this pleasure, egocentrism would be its *raison d'être*, and pleasure, not joy, would describe the community's tone of life. But with benevolent self-transcending into the vulnerable, needy and beautiful life of the other comes a joyful existence.

I have distinguished the satisfaction that characterizes the life of faith (joy) from everyday, egocentric pleasures. Does such a distinction contain a suppressed asceticism – an implication that faith has nothing to do with ordinary pleasures, including the pleasures of aesthetic world engagements? Here we recall an earlier point: to be empathetically (joyfully) drawn into the world of the other does not repudiate or suppress the needs and desires of natural egocentrism, only their idolatrous distortion. Rather, the redemptive remaking of human desires assimilates natural egocentrism into ethical self-transcendence – that is, into responsibility.[13] The reason why ethical self-transcendence does not simply abolish natural egocentrism is that its very function is to break the power of its anxious, idolatrous attachments. Thus, it transforms but does not abolish the *desire* and need structure of human life. Freed from idolatrous attachments, the human being empathetically acknowledges the legitimacy, goodness, and distinctive reality of any and all others. To acknowledge another entity in this way is to grant, apprehend and enjoy its autonomy, complexity and its mixture of pathos and beauty. Thus, the human being is opened not only on to the consenting, self-surpassing beauty of human others but on to beauty as being. Accordingly, ethical self-transcendence and the joy of sympathetic participation in the other's beauty is the ground of faith's hedonistic dimension, its orientation to the beauty of being and the legitimation of the needs and desires of natural egocentrism and its world engagements. Acknowledged and valued is the beautiful, graceful body and its efficient, fluid, spontaneous actions. Acknowledged as authentic are world engagements which apprehend not only static harmonies but the accomplished syntheses of temporal flow. Certain Psalms express the 'properness' and beauty of the world: 'At the works of thy hands I sing for joy' (Psalm 92.4); 'Praise the Lord from the earth, you sea monsters and all deeps, fire and hail, snow and frost' (Psalm 148:7–8). The theme also persists in hymns and prayers: 'For the joy of ear and eye, for the heart and mind's delight, for the mystic harmony linking sense to sound and sight.'[14]

Is it not a risk to open the doors of faith to egocentric pleasures? Once pleasures are granted a valued status, might they not take over the life of faith, returning redemptive existence to the dynamics of utility and egocentric need? It would be foolish to insist that this cannot happen. After all, do we not see this happen in virtually every period and type of religion? Any and all good things, especially those that call forth intense pleasures, carry with them the same risk. But we remind ourselves that what is under consideration is faith and the life of faith. Insofar as that is our subject, we must say that beauty and the aesthetic, joy and pleasure, are phenomena of redemptive transformation. They arise out of, and with, ethical self-transcendence. This means that a joyful tone of participation, the pleasures of the world's beauty and the satisfactions of pleasurable experience all take place within, and not outside, responsibility. In redemption the pleasurable existence of natural egocentrism becomes a part of ethical self-transcending relations with human and non-human others. Accordingly, one enjoys nature's beauties in connection with empathetic responsibility for nature. This is not to say that the beautiful is simply subject to the moral. The aesthetic is irreducible to anything else. To admit beauty into one's life only if it serves a 'moral' purpose would be to destroy it. Yet it is ethical self-transcendence (redemption) that restores the *imago Dei* and opens the human being to beauty, and this means that sensibility to beauty is a sensibility of ethical self-transcendence. It flows from consent, participation and empathy, not from autonomy, self-survival or self-securing. Paradoxically, this apparent limitation of beauty is the condition of beauty's authentic autonomy. Without it, human beings are prone to 'use' the beautiful to exorcize their demons.

Faith without Beauty

Our inquiry nears its end. Its conclusion is that, as self-transcending, compassionate benevolence and as a joyful sensibility to the mysteries and pathetic harmonies of the world, faith is beautiful. But history has made it clear that this aesthetic dimension of faith can be suppressed, and even removed, from language by certain kinds of pieties, casuistries and theologies. In some forms of the Christian movement, beauty and, with it, the pleasurable enjoyment of the world, has been identified with egocentrism, carnality and sin. The result is a severe impoverishment of individual, communal and churchly life. Four forms of this impoverishment are historically familiar: alienation from nature, bodily asceticism, legalism and literalism. All four impoverish the life of faith and, with it, human life by effecting a dulled perception, an aborted way of acting in the world, and by reducing human self-transcendence.

Alienation from nature is now a familiar theme in writings that call for a new ecological and environmental responsibility. These texts accuse modern industrialized nations of risking the health of the whole biosphere (as well as the existence of many species of flora and fauna) by their policies of land use, agro-businesses, pesticides and energy sources. They also contend that centuries-long ways of thinking about nature, some of which were prompted by Western Christianity, are at the root of relations to nature that lack all elements of responsibility. Others have pointed out that urbanization and technology together have produced styles of modern life that distance human beings from nature. Of course, it is an exaggeration to blame the Christian movement for all the planet's ecological problems; widespread industrialization, out-of-control population expansion and tendencies at work in other religious faiths must share the blame. Yet, the Christian movement has spawned ways of thinking that contribute to modern alienations from nature. Despite the belief that God is 'maker of heaven and earth', Christian piety and theology have rarely accorded nature a very important place. I suspect that this marginalization of nature is perpetuated by the marginalization of beauty. The fear of 'aestheticism' and 'natural theology' has prompted piety and theology to be suspicious of beauty and suppress it from the life of faith, the result being an undermining of the way in which redemptive transformation orients the human being to joy and to pleasurable relations with the mysterious, pathetic and beautiful natural world. Nature then disappears as a legitimate and important location of human experience and responsibility.

Bodily asceticism, or alienation from the body, is a second form of impoverishment in that it denies faith its aesthetic aspect. Bodily asceticism entered early Christianity from religious movements of the East and the Mediterranean basin, perhaps finding an opening by way of a martyrdom spirituality. Narrowly defined bodily asceticism means self-imposed bodily disciplines, as well as deprivations of the natural bodily needs of food, sleep, comfort, sexual activity and self-imposed bodily disciplines. Through these bodily self-denials, ascetics suffer for their sins, reduce human autonomy and self-focus, and create conditions for self-transcending contemplation and spirituality. In a broader sense, bodily asceticism is a piety and casuistry that regards human desires for comfort, pleasure, entertainment and self-satisfaction as obstacles to faith and piety.

It is important not to identify bodily asceticism, narrow or broad, with the self-sacrifices and disciplines incurred by the human being's attempt to live and act responsibly in situations of conflict, politics, persecution and crisis. In the life and teachings of Jesus, we find the latter and not the former. To punish and deprive the desiring body simply because it is desiring assumes that natural egocentrism itself is evil. Further, absent in bodily asceticism is any notion of the legitimacy of pleasure – a notion that would expel the aesthetic from the life of faith.[15] If the human being's formal and ethical self-transcendence is a reflection of what is divine, then its apparatus of self and desire, including the body (the field of its experience and activity) is not suppressed and abolished by redemption but transformed and released into its proper function. Redemption thus restores the disposition of beauty present in nascent form in the imago and bestows on its ongoing life both joy and pleasure. Accordingly, bodily asceticism, in the sense of a repudiation of the self and its desires, curtails a whole dimension of redemptive transformation.

Legalism and its partner, moralism, is a third impoverishment of faith brought about by the suppression of beauty. Legalism, a phenomenon closely tied to a forensic way of understanding faith, is what happens to human obligation when it reduces itself to, or wholly defines itself by, specific ordinances.[16] The result is that the primary object or referent of obligation shifts from the vulnerable other to a system of taboos and requirements. Legalism can also dominate the piety of a religious community, thus creating institutional structures and paradigms of interpretation. In a legalist paradigm, the primary point of the Gospel is the prospect of future reward and punishment and the conditions of obtaining the one and avoiding the other. Oral or written ordinances and a juridical system of enforcement provide the primary metaphor for God's redemptive activity, the significance of the event and person of Jesus, and the central point of the whole drama of redemption. In that paradigm God's primary relation to human beings in history is righteous demand, punishment and reward. The primary meaning of the event of Jesus is the bringing about of the conditions for changing impending punishment into reward. And the central point of the Gospel is the procuring, by way of forensic judgement, a heavenly rather than an infernal destiny. In the forensic paradigm of redemption, concern for a 'just' and balanced outcome suppresses the remaking of the divine image and, with that, the redemption that draws the human being into ethical self-transcendence and into empathetic sensibility to the beautiful pathos of the other. Self-transcending sensibility to the beautiful other does not determine the quality of mutuality in the faith community. The other as pathetically beautiful recedes behind a complex structure of moral conventions and its forensic paradigm. In that paradigm conformity to ordinances and to right beliefs, concern for proper enforcement and focus on the egocentric project of obtaining the right forensic status that guarantees a heavenly destiny take centre stage in the community. In other words, the legalist paradigm of faith repeats the distortions of the imago effected by sin.

Literalism is a fourth way in which the suppression of beauty impoverishes the life of faith. Many things constitute the life of faith, interpretation being one of them. For faith or redemptive existence never comes about in a historical and linguistic vacuum but from specific traditions passed on in the form of narratives, rituals and sacred writings. Believers exist in the world by way of 'official' traditions of interpretation embodied in the community which they constantly reinterpret as they live from the community's narrative tradition in ordinary situations of life. Hermeneutics, then, is not simply an arcane possession of the religious community's professional interpreters. Literalism names what appears to be an ever-recurring corruption of interpretation in the religious community. Its roots are the egocentric need for certainty and the idolatrous tendency to make human words, ideas and metaphors coincide with, or exhaustively express, the mystery of the sacred. As a flawed form of interpretation, literalism represents an insensibility to the multiple layers of meaning, the metaphorical character, the hidden political and cultural strata and the mysterious horizon of all human language. Literalism is a pseudo-hermeneutics because it is not so much interpretation as the denial of the need for interpretation. The notion that the words of a text are God's own linguistic formulation presupposes that God has interpreted the text by simply delivering it. Accordingly, it is not self-evident to the literalist why a text requires interpretation at all.

The phenomenon of literalistic (non)interpretation in a religious community or its individuals does seem connected to the suppression of beauty. We recall that one effect of redemptive self-transcendence is to open and orient the human being first to the beautiful reality of the vulnerable other and, by this means, to the mixture of harmony and pathos in all things. To be engaged with the entities and events of the world in this way is to be summoned into their mystery, unexplained depths and surplus meanings. And to apprehend things in this way is at the same time to grasp the various ways in which they over-flow language. When beauty is suppressed, that which overflows language (the world's mystery and complexity) is also suppressed. Furthermore, the languages of interpretation tend to have built-in devices that make the inter-preter aware of this overflow, devices of qualification, negation and metaphor. To interpret is to have some sensibility to these devices. Lacking this sensibility, the literalist will miss the nuances, ambiguities, settings and deep strata that mark all texts. This is why literalism is an impoverishment of an important aspect of the life of faith.

Arts in the Life of Faith

Throughout this inquiry I have reminded the reader that our subject is beauty in the life of faith, not religion and the arts. Accordingly, I have tried to reveal how beauty is part of the way in which the faithful person behaves towards others and in the world. I have not attempted to articulate how the arts are part of the life of faith or religious community. Whatever the importance of the arts in the history of the religious community, they are not the primary means by which beauty persists in the life of faith, for beauty is always already present in the *imago Dei* and its redemptive restoration and it already shapes the world as being. Yet strange would be a theological aesthetic that totally ignored the arts. Just because beauty is primordial to human experience, human beings from prehistory to the present have found ways of acting out, sounding out, painting or writing the aesthetic dimension of their experience into enduring forms.[17] These reproductions of the world's rhythms, sounds, colours and shapes call into existence a duplication of beauty as being. Present and at work in human communities are not only the sounds, colours and shapes of woods, skies and animals but all these things re-imagined in works of art.[18] The same holds for religious communities. They do not remember, praise or celebrate an abstract and formless sacred: they dance, pipe and narrate the sacred by way of the beautiful body, the musical instrument and the oral or written story. Even though arts are not themselves the origin, or even the primary mediation, of beauty in the life of faith, neither are they trivial in the communities of faith.

Once we acknowledge the importance of the arts to religious communities and human cultures, we confront a certain ambiguity in the term, 'the arts'. In the texts of Western history, art (*techné, ars*) has had a variety of meanings: skilled activity, (for example, the art of living), anything requiring teaching and learning, a select group of highly valued activities (music, poetry), the seven 'liberal arts' of the Middle Ages. According to Paul O. Kristeller, the 'modern system of the arts' (painting, sculpture, architecture, music and poetry) arose in the eighteenth century.[19] With this nucleus, plus certain satellite arts of dance, theatre and engraving came the notion of 'high arts', and thus the hierarchy of *the* arts in contrast to crafts, folk arts and technology. Kristeller, Ortega y Gasset and others have also traced the decline of the concept of 'high arts' in the twentieth century in which trends within the old nucleus group, plus the emergence of new arts, blurred the boundary between the 'high arts' and the arts of popular culture. The point here is that the very concept of *the* arts is historically variable and culturally determined. Hence, when we take up the question of *arts* in the life of faith, are we asking how the 'high arts' figure into faith, theology or the religious community? My inclination is not to permit the old nucleus of high arts to set the question of arts in the life of faith. But once we embark on this broadened path, we face a new problem – the status of the 'arts' of a consumer society and its mass culture. Power, hierarchy, elitism and patronage have always had a function in the arts of both the East and West, but marketing and consumer societies of the postmodern West seem to have produced a new phenomenon. Aggressively marketed music, poster art, movies, television and certain kinds of novel are neither 'high arts' nor 'folk arts' in the sense of individually produced and locally oriented, craft-like works. In the analysis that follows, the term 'arts' includes both 'high' and 'folk' art but not the 'arts' of consumer-driven mass culture.[20]

A second ambiguity posed by the term 'the arts' has to do with the relationship between arts and beauty. Traditional works in aesthetics more or less correlated the two, thus allowing beauty to define the arts. It is fair to say that virtually no contemporary theory of the arts (or perhaps even artist) would grant beauty such a powerful status. In the new consensus, a work need not be beautiful to be an authentic work of art.[21] What gives it artistic authenticity is something broader than beauty. The authentic work of art can bring into form (or non-form) what is disturbing, oppressive, frightening, ugly or meaningless – possibly something that has little or no relation to the world at all.[22] We can grant the point. Engendering something beautiful need not be the artist's primary aim. Do we thereby also grant to the artist an utter indifference to beauty, a complete absence of beauty as a trait of authentic art? Here the issue becomes complicated. If beauty is being – that is, if beauty is intrinsic to any and all determinate, differentiated, continuous sights, sounds, entities and processes, it will be irrepressible even in art. The photographer may capture on film a trash heap in an urban alley or the final moments of a starving child. But if the photographer works as an artist, she or he will so photograph these things that their 'ugly' and pathetic content will constitute a self-transcending experience for the observer. Is that experience simply one of ugliness, entirely reducible to the photograph's shocking, disgusting contents?[23] I suggest that ugly and even shocking subjects are able to disturb because, as being, their contents are never ugly in their totality. Even as the pathos of the finite shows through all beautiful things, so beauty ever hovers on the edge of the ugly because the ugly suggests what contrasts to it. Furthermore, the ugly is never mere chaos. If it were, it would have no determinacy at all. In order to display what shocks, grieves or disgusts, the artist is bound to what is necessary for expression (geometrical shapes, musical transitions, linguistic devices). And all determinate expression evokes being. The wasteland may be ugly; T.S. Eliot's poem is not. The devastating battle may be horrifying but Picasso's *Guernica* is not mere ugliness: its very horror depends on the viewer's ability to contrast it to non-suffering and non-brutality. Beauty will emerge even in the beauty-indifferent artist (if there is such a person). To display anything at all – even the most abstract and apparently chaotic entity – artists as craftpersons must engage the world by way of its resonances, colours, sounds and languages. Even if beauty has lost its power to be the all-inclusive and defining criterion of authentic art, it still remains a *sine qua non* – something that trails along with the artist's means of display. And insofar as the artist's effort is not merely abstract but depicts any piece of the world or world engagement, beauty inserts itself.

Arts in the Christian Church (church architecture, painting, sculpture, music and the poetic aspects of the Bible and other writings) have been the subject of detailed historical investigation. I shall make no attempt to reproduce that sort of inquiry. Granting the historical fact and importance of art in the history of the various Churches, I would pose a question that arises naturally from the subject of this book. If beauty is an intrinsic aspect of the life of faith as I have contended, in what way might the life of faith intersect with the arts?

Such a question prompts an initial and rather obvious answer. If faith (redemptive self-transcendence) disposes the human being towards any and all beauty, that disposal will not restrict itself simply to nature or the human other but will be engaged by the ambiguous beauty of works of art. In other words, if redemptive self-transcendence calls forth a general disposition towards beauty, that disposition will not exclude the arts. A possible implication of the thesis is that it explains the presence of the arts in the history of the worshipping community. When people write texts, build buildings and sing songs, beauty will reveal itself. There is a certain self-evidence about this initial response that I have no inclination to dispute. On the other hand, this response does little more than connect a general orientation to beauty brought about by faith with the presence of the arts in the religious community. Here we are prompted to take another step.

Let us recall the individual and societal distortion of the divine image. Wounded in its formal and ethical self-transcendence, the divine image takes on a distorted relation to beauty, displayed in a dulled sensitivity (Philistinism) or an aesthetic idolatry. It is difficult to imagine that such distortions have no effect on the way in which human beings relate to, and pursue, the arts. In a given place and time, both the arts themselves and their way of functioning in society and in the lives of individuals can be shaped by Philistinism and aestheticism.[24] We recall at this point that redemptive transformation or ethical self-transcendence reshapes the human orientation to beauty by opening it to beauty's pathetic aspect. This reshaping reduces the inclination to suppress or merely manipulate beauty or reduce beauty to the pretty. It would seem then that a reshaped relation to beauty, born in the joy of interhuman participation and broadened to other aesthetic pleasures, would somehow affect the human being's distorted relation to the arts. For what ethical self-transcendence apprehends in the work of art is also what it apprehends in the work of nature – the beautiful, vulnerable 'face' of finite entities in all their mystery, peril and promise. Artists – perhaps despite themselves and beyond their conscious intentions – negotiate this 'face' as they bring their work to display. The most successful of them have found a way of displaying the world's enchantments, surprises, unpredictabilities, complexities and mysteries. Such a display requires a kind of ethical self-transcendence, and the resulting work of art engages the ethically self-transcendent interpreter.

And now a final point. If a reshaped divine image does affect one's relation to beauty and, through that, one's relation to the arts, it would seem that these reshapings would influence how the arts form part of the Christian community. If beauty is being, beauty will emerge in everything the religious community does: in its Scriptures, rituals, sacred spaces and icons. But beauty's powerful presence in the life of faith adds another dimension. In the life of faith, what is primarily beautiful is the act and disposition of benevolent consent to any and all things. Such an act is at the very core of the Christian Gospel, and it finds its way into every Christian theme: the self-sacrificial Messiah, the creation, the *imago Dei*, and even what constitutes the ecclesia. The primary beauty of ethical self-transcendence is the lens through which the believer apprehends the Gospel and, beyond that, the world. Benevolently beautiful is the world-maker which spins the world into existence and pursues its redemption. Here we have the primary criterion for how the religious community draws the arts into its corporate life. This criterion is what prevents 'religious arts' from being simply a miscellany of pedagogical devices. Rather, the primordial beauty of benevolence must find some expression in every artistic thematization: in Jesus, Mary, the world, a biblical incident. 'Christian art', then, constantly searches for linguistic, musical and architectural ways of expressing the narrative themes of redemption. But what constitutes the beauty of these themes is self-transcending, pathetic, consenting benevolence.

Notes

1   Walter de la Mare, 'Shadow', *Collected Poems* (London: Faber and Faber, 1979), p. 24.
2   Dante, *The Divine Comedy, 3, Paradise*, trans. Dorothy Sayers and Barbara Reynolds (Harmondsworth: Penguin Books, 1962), Canto XXXI, line 133.
3   Ibid., Canto XXXIII, line 191.
4   Aristotle's term for the presupposed principle of differentiation and the sub-stratum of change was *hyle*, matter.
5   Søren Kierkegaard is one of the few philosophers who sensed an element of pathos in beauty itself. But it is not the aesthetic but the ethical orientation that apprehends this. For there is a certain sadness or melancholy that attends the struggles of living things and human beings for life – a struggle which itself is beautiful.
6   Gilbert Keith Chesterton, 'Ecclesiastes', *The Collected Poems of G.K. Chesterton* (New York: Dodd, Mead and Co., 1911), p. 310.
7   Ernest Becker, *The Denial of Death* (New York: Free Press Paperbacks, 1997).
8   Vassar Miller, 'For a Spiritual Mentor', *If I Had Wheels or Love: Collected Poems of Vassar Miller* (Dallas, Texas: Southern Methodist University Press, 1991), p. 251.
9   For a historical account of the rigorist strand of Christian piety and religious life, see Kenneth E. Kirk, *The Vision of God: The Christian Doctrine of the Summum Bonum* (London: Longmans Green, 1932).
10   Christopher Lasch, *The Culture of Narcissism: American Life in an Age of Diminished Expectations* (New York: Norton, 1978).
11   Gerard Manley Hopkins, 'The Windhover (to Christ our Lord)', *Poems of Gerard Manley Hopkins* (London: Oxford University Press, 1930), p. 29.
12   A particular line of late twentieth-century philosophy of religion and theology has explored the relationship between the ethical (cf. ethical self-transcendence) and joy. Informed by the philosophy of the late Emmanuel Levinas, Edith Wyschogrod and David Ford, both have extended Levinas's radical account of responsibility by way of the motif of joy. Joy is an important theme of David Ford's work on 'self and salvation'. Dialogue with selected texts is his method of approaching and thinking about joy. He extracts insights from Dietrich Bonhoeffer, Eberhard Jüngel, Edith Wyschogrod and Therese of Lisieux. The result is an account of 'joyful responsibility'. Accordingly, the human response to God is not simply one of responsibility but a 'rejoicing in God for God's own sake' (Jüngel), and the celebratory excess of worship. Thus, joyful, worshipful responsibility shapes one's daily life with others. Joy, then, in Ford's interpretation, is not reducible to narcissism or pleasure but can be a self-transcending joy in others. See David Ford, *Self and Salvation: Being Transformed* (Cambridge: Cambridge University Press, 1999).
13   Søren Kierkegaard expressed this point by claiming that the ethical sphere does not necessarily suppress or exclude the aesthetic. Rather, the ethical imparts a higher beauty to everything. Since the ethical means 'personality concentrated in itself', it does not displace the aesthetic: 'Equilibrium Between the Aesthetical and the Ethical', *Either-Or: A Fragment of Life*, Vol. II, trans. David and Lillian Swenson (Princeton, NJ: Princeton University Press, 1941), p. 210ff.
14   From the hymn by Conrad Kocher, 'For the Beauty of the Earth' (1838).
15   'A Christian having renounced the world, its power and pleasure, cannot seek pleasure for itself, nor diversion for the sake of diversion.' Mortimer Adler quotes here from a seventeenth-century anti-theatre figure, Count de Conti. See *Art and Prudence: A Study of Practical Philosophy* (New York: Longmans Green and Co., 1937).
16   For an elaboration of this point, see the author's *Deep Symbols: Their Postmodern Effacement and Reclamation* (Valley Forge, PA: Trinity Press International, 1996), Chapter 6.
17   For a study of the arts in archaic cultures, see Gerardus van der Leeuw, *Sacred and Profane Beauty: The Holy in Art*, trans. David E. Green (New York: Holt, Rinehart and Winston, 1963), Part Three, Chapter 1; Part Four, Chapter 2.
18   This link between the work of art and many worlds of human experience does not carry with it the thesis that duplicating natural objects is the primary function of art, an often criticized theory.

19 See Paul Oscar Kristeller, *Renaissance Thought II* (Princeton, NJ: Princeton University Press, 1980), Chapter IX, I.

20 For a powerful case on behalf of the authenticity and importance of crafts and folk arts, see Coetsu Yanagi's *The Unknown Craftsman: A Japanese Insight into Beauty* (Kodansha International Ltd, 1972). Yanagi was the founder of the craft movement in Japan and also of the Japan Folkcraft Museum. He laboured both in Japan and Korea for the preservation of folk art and for the support of craft artists.

21 The link between the arts and beauty has not been entirely severed in twentieth-century aesthetic theory. See, for instance, Herbert Marcuse, *The Aesthetic Dimension: Toward a Critique of Marxist Aesthetics* (Boston: Beacon Press, 1978), p. v; Nicholas Wolterstorff, *Art in Action*, Chapter 4, p. 3; and Mikel Dufrenne, 'Introduction', *The Phenomenology of Aesthetic Experience*, trans. E. Casey (Evanston, IL: Northwestern University Press, 1973). In Dufrenne's view, while beauty is not a norm for the aesthetic object, it can be used for the 'fullness (and meaning) of sensuous being', 'the authenticity of the work of art', and 'the true made visible' (p. ix).

22 For a study of the differences between the 'old art' (with its core of lived reality and link to human experience) and 'new art' (with its irony, play and dehumanization), see Ortega y Gassett, 'On the Dehumanization of Art', in *On the Dehumanization of Art and Other Essays on Art, Culture, and Literature* (Princeton, NJ: Princeton University Press, 1948).

23 For a discussion of arts that make the 'ugly' their theme and subject matter and arts that would present a 'deformation of reality', see Herbert Read, 'Beauty and the Beast', in *On Beauty* (Dallas: Spring Publications, 1987).

24 Two severe critics of the twentieth-century art of both the capitalist (European, American) and communist world were George Steiner and Herbert Marcuse. Steiner painted a grim picture of the arts in the consumer, bureaucratic societies in which the paraphernalia of 'scholarly' and other reinterpretations displaced the engagements and immediacies of the arts with a 'paper Leviathan of secondary talk': *Real Presences* (Chicago: University of Chicago Press, 1989), p. 48. Marcuse contended that all arts are radically critical, creative and transcending of any and all social forms and political agendas, including revolution itself. To harness the arts to revolutionary agendas was to tame and destroy them. See Herbert Marcuse, *The Aesthetic Dimension: Toward a Critique of Marxist Aesthetics* (Boston: Beacon Press, 1978).

Synopsis

Aesthetics

'Aesthetic' refers to an aspect of human experience evoked by an immediate relation to what is beautiful – that is, with what draws human beings into self-transcending and non-useful satisfactions. 'Aesthetics' refers to a branch of philosophy or art criticism whose task is to understand the unity and features of works of art and the experience of art. Beauty occupies a central or defining place in aesthetic inquiry and only a secondary and non-defining place in aesthetics.

A 'theological aesthetic' seeks to understand the place of beauty in the life of faith: a 'theological aesthetics' seeks to understand the place of the arts in the religious community.

Beauty

Beauty (the aesthetic) is not among the primary values or deep symbols of postmodern societies, nor has it had a central place in the symbols, pieties and theologies of most of the branches of Christianity. Certain features of postmodern society (isolation from nature, technocratic and bureaucratic institutions, consumerism and cultural narcissism) tend to diminish beauty both as an important value and as an interpretive concept.

Contributing to the postmodern effacement of beauty is a hermeneutic legacy, a tradition of interpretation, governed by dichotomies between the ethical and the aesthetic, religion (faith) and the aesthetic, and religion (faith) and pleasure.

Accordingly, a contemporary aesthetic (or theological aesthetic) that seeks to restore beauty as important to human experience or religious faith faces the deconstructive task of exposing and breaking down these dichotomies. The displacement of the aesthetic by aesthetics (philosophy of the arts) in recent times has contributed to the suppression of beauty in hermeneutics, philosophy and criticism.

A contemporary theological aesthetic also works in the setting of a centuries-long marginalization – in some cases suppression – of the aesthetic by Hebraic and Christian iconoclasm, asceticism and legalism. While beauty was always a part of the Christian cultus through the poetry of language (in Scriptures, liturgies and devotional writings), architecture, sculpture, icons and music, it remained marginal to its pieties, hermeneutics (principles of interpretation), and moral and doctrinal theologies.

The suppression of beauty in the Christian movement severely impoverishes faith and piety in four principal ways: the discrediting of world-related satisfactions by bodily asceticism, alienation from nature, legalist modes of life that reduce piety to conformity, and literalisms that eliminate sensibility to nuance, metaphor and mystery.

The Western Story of Beauty

Twenty-five hundred years of texts constitute a Western 'story of beauty' whose variety both renders the term 'beauty' ambiguous and provides mutually supplementing insights into beauty's elusive complexity.

A historical examination of the Western story of beauty provides a more varied and fruitful route to the character of beauty than formal definition or phenomenological description.

Four interpretations of beauty are especially prominent in the Western story of beauty: 'the great theory of beauty' as proportion or harmony (classical Hellenism and the Middle Ages), beauty as a sensibility (eighteenth-century England), beauty as consenting benevolence (Jonathan Edwards) and beauty as a self-transcending and transcendental dimension of experience (Kant, Schopenhauer).

The Western story of beauty is not simply a discredited or antiquated tradition but, rather, a legacy of insights available to contemporary inquiry, criticism and interpretation.

From the Western story of beauty we learn the following:

1   Since all forms and actualities are never sheer chaos but instead are instances of particularity, content, continuity, differentiation and pattern, to be – either as abstract form or actual entity or event – is to be beautiful.
2   Chaos (non-being), however, is never simply absent from beauty, but rather persists in all beautiful things as what is not totally patterned, as matter, chance, structural incompatibility, passing away or entropic decline into sameness. Since these elements of chaos are always a part of what is actual and always attend unity, variety, pattern, the grace of movement and the like, every beautiful entity has an element of pathos.
3   Beauty as formed, patterned unity in differentiation evokes from any and all experiencing creatures some degree of satisfaction. In the human sphere, satisfaction that comes with the structure of experience itself can vary in intensity, and can take the form either of a dulled or intensified sensibility.
4   Because the attractiveness and satisfaction of harmony or proportion draws the human being out of its self-preoccupation into self-transcendence, what is beautiful is never merely the servant of the managing and 'useful' activities of natural egocentrism.
5   The primary (most attractive, most satisfying) instance of beauty is not the harmonized difference of finite entities but a self-transcending disposition of benevolent caring (Edwards). All beauty evokes a transcendence towards the beautiful, but primary beauty is an ethical, empathetic self-transcendence.

Theological Aesthetics and Redemptive Transformation

Theological aesthetics (the theology of the arts) presupposes a theological aesthetic (a theology of the aesthetic dimension of the life of faith).

The most direct theological route to the presence and motif of beauty is not a natural theology that discovers finite beauty's analogical dependence on divine beauty, nor is it an analysis of one or more doctrines (creation, Spirit, sacrament), but rather is an inquiry into what all doctrinal motifs presuppose – the fact of redemption itself.

A theological aesthetic works to uncover the way faith – that is, individual and corporate existence transformed by redemption – is beautiful and gives rise to sensibilities to beauty.

While it is certainly the case that the primordial foundation of beauty is God's self-surpassing, creative benevolence, theology's initial access to beauty is the beauty that redemption brings – the beauty of faith itself.

Because redemptive remaking presupposes that the human being *needs* to be remade (because of sin or evil) and that it is *remakable* (the *imago Dei*), redemption possesses the triadic structure of the divine image, the corruption of the divine image by sin, and redemptive transformation. If a theology fails to discern beauty in this triadic structure, it will exclude or marginalize beauty when it interprets piety, spirituality, culture and ethics.

Redemptive transformation can be beautiful and can engender sensibilities to beauty only if a primordial beauty already describes the human being as the *imago Dei*.

Because the divine image is the human being's resemblance to God, it is at the same time that which is corrupted by sin or human evil. The divine image presupposed both by sin and redemptive remaking is both a *formal* self-transcendence (thus, the human being is not simply an inert, passive, thing-like being) and an *ethical* self-transcendence (thus, the human being is constituted to surpass itself in caring consent to what is other). Sin presupposes, and redemption restores, both distorted formal self-transcendence (formal freedom) and distorted ethical self-transcendence.

Sin's alteration of benevolent self-transcendence into idolatrous self-securing distorts the beauty of the divine image in a twofold way: first, it reduces sensibility to the beauty of any and all others (Philistinism); second, it makes the world's beauty a mere function of human self-securing (aestheticism).

The four motifs or paradigms of beauty in the Western story of beauty (beauty as being, sensibility, self-transcendence and benevolence) help theology understand and articulate how beauty is present in the life of faith.

1   Ethical self-transcendence or benevolence is beautiful both in its nascent form of the *imago Dei* and in redemptive re-making.

2   Ethical self-transcendence opens the human being empathetically to the reality, distinctive difference and pathos of any and all others, and this generates an enduring sensibility to beauty as being.

3   The redemptive remaking of the divine image restores both the freedoms

that constitute formal and ethical self-transcendence, and thus draws the human being beyond mere egocentrism, self-preoccupation and self-securing.

4   Finite beauty (and possibly the beauty of God) includes both the chaos element ever present in and with being and the pathos that comes with compassionate benevolence.

Insofar as redemptive transformation effects a courageous freedom able to consent to chaos and the tragic without idols, it frees the human being to accept and participate in the pathos and, with that, in the beauty of the world.

Because redemptive transformation creates or restores a sensibility to the beauty of any and all others, it constitutes a hedonistic aspect – an orientation to satisfaction and pleasure – in the life of faith.

Because the sensibility to beauty (intrinsic satisfaction) in the life of faith is rooted in consenting, benevolent ethical self-transcendence towards any and all others, the life of faith is neither a conflict between, nor a mere amalgam of, orientations towards pleasure and orientations of responsibility. The pleasurable sensibility to beauty is taken up into, and is part of, self-transcending benevolence.

While the orientation to what is intrinsically beautiful opens the human being (and the religious community) to all beautiful things and therefore to the arts, the caring benevolence of redemptive existence engenders a distinctive way in which art can be 'religious art' – that is, art in service of faith and worship in the life of the worshipping community.

Index